The Breast Cancer Prevention Plan

20 Proven Steps for Reducing Your Breast Cancer Risk

DR. EDWARD J. CONLEY

McGraw·Hill

New York   Chicago   San Francisco   Lisbon   London   Madrid   Mexico City
Milan   New Delhi   San Juan   Seoul   Singapore   Sydney   Toronto

Library of Congress Cataloging-in-Publication Data

Conley, Edward J.
   The breast cancer prevention plan: 20 proven steps for reducing
your breast cancer risk/by Edward J. Conley.
      p. cm.
   Includes index.
   ISBN 0-07-146387-9 (alk. paper)
      1. Breast—Cancer—Prevention—Popular works. 2.
   Breast—Cancer—Risk factors—Popular works. 3. Middle aged
   women—Health and hygiene—Popular works. I. Title.
      RA645.C3C654 2006
      616.99'449—dc22

                                           2005014313

1 2 3 4 5 6 7 8 9 0   DOC/DOC   0 9 8 7 6 5

ISBN 0-07-146387-9

McGraw-Hill books are available at special quantity discounts to use as premiums and
sales promotions, or for use in corporate training programs. For more information, please
write to the Director of Special Sales, Professional Publishing, McGraw-Hill, Two Penn
Plaza, New York, NY 10121-2298. Or contact your local bookstore.

The information contained in this book is intended to provide helpful and informative
material on the subject addressed. It is not intended to serve as a replacement for professional medical advice. Any use of the information in this book is at the reader's dis-
cretion. The author and publisher specifically disclaim any and all liability arising directly
or indirectly from the use or application of any information contained in this book.
A health-care professional should be consulted regarding your specific condition.

Contents

Introduction

I have written this book to share with you vital information that can dramatically improve your quality of life and possibly save you (and your family) from breast cancer. This information is not commonly available and even your doctor may not know many of the "secrets" we will discuss. In this book you will learn:

- That only 20 to 30 percent of breast cancer is inherited.
- That 70 to 80 percent of breast cancer is *avoidable.*
- How traditional estrogen replacement therapy (ERT) increases your breast cancer risk.
- How a safer estrogen named *estriol* can control menopausal symptoms with much less risk.
- The easy and inexpensive tests that best predict if you are going to get breast cancer in the future.
- How to improve your EMI (estrogen metabolite index) and your EQ (estrogen quotient) score to dramatically lower your breast cancer risk.
- Which chemicals you eat everyday that damage your breasts and how to avoid or neutralize them.
- Delicious and inexpensive foods that may cut breast cancer risk in *half*!
- Natural antioxidants that protect your breasts from the damage that causes breast cancer.

- Best of all: How to combine all of these "secrets" into a dynamic program that may cut your breast cancer risk by 90 percent!

THE ESTROGEN CONTROVERSY

On July 17, 2002, the estrogen bubble broke. It was reported in the *Journal of the American Medical Association* that the Woman's Health Initiative Study (WHI) was halted due to an unacceptable increase in breast cancer for women on conjugated estrogen (0.625 milligrams) and medroxyprogesterone (2.5 milligrams), the two most common forms of hormone replacement.[1] Nearly 69 million prescriptions had been written for Premarin (conjugated estrogen) and Prempro (conjugated estrogen plus medroxyprogesterone), making conjugated estrogen the second most prescribed medication in the U.S. and accounting for over one billion dollars in sales. The WHI results caused nearly 65 percent of women on estrogen replacement therapy to stop their therapy. While many of these women felt relatively good after going off of ERT, millions of women felt miserable. They had sleep disturbances, night sweats, hot flashes, depression, mood swings, fatigue, incontinence, sexual dysfunction, and a dramatic drop in their quality of life. In fact, up to 25 percent of these women have now gone back on their ERT despite the greater risk of developing breast cancer.[2] What these women don't know, is that there is a safer estrogen, that has been used in Europe for fifty years, that controls menopausal symptoms but does not appear to increase the risk of breast cancer. That estrogen is named Estriol, and in later chapters we will discuss what it is, why it's safer, how to get it, how to use it, and what to tell your doctor.

TESTS THAT BEST PREDICT
BREAST CANCER

There are also simple and inexpensive—but woefully under-prescribed—tests that are the best predictors of who will get breast cancer in the future. Remember the mammogram, while important, only tells you if you have breast cancer at the time of the test, it says next to nothing about if you will get breast cancer in the future. These tests that assess your real risk are named the *Estrogen Metabolite Index* (EMI) and the *Estrogen Quotient* (EQ). They are easy urine tests that studies show are the best predictor of whether or not you are going to get breast cancer in the future. Knowing your real risk will help you determine how you should monitor your health in the future. Every woman should know her EMI and EQ score! Even if your score on either of these tests are low and you are at increased risk of breast cancer, there are natural ways to improve your EMI and EQ and dramatically lower your risk. It's important to note, too, that most American doctors do not know about these tests.

EASY STEPS YOU CAN TAKE
TO AVOID BREAST CANCER

Over the next decade, 2 million American women will get breast cancer and about 400,000 will die. You don't have to be one of them! In this book, we will present a plan that consists of 20 easy, inexpensive, and medically proven "secrets" you can use to dramatically lower the risk that you will get breast cancer. This plan includes delicious foods and natural supplements that help protect your breasts from the damage that causes breast cancer. Even if you don't follow every step, just starting with one or two may allow you to cut your breast cancer risk and ensure you never hear those horrible words "You Have Breast Cancer."

WHY YOUR DOCTOR
DOESN'T KNOW THIS

On 9/11 we learned a painful lesson: that it's much better to prevent a terrorist attack than fight a war after the fact! Unfortunately American medicine is still stuck in the old way of thinking. We are trained to fight a "war" on cancer after you have it! No one would argue that we need to continue to find new and better treatments for breast cancer, but the truth is plain: *The best treatment for breast cancer is to never get it in the first place!* In the next ten years, 2 million American women and countless millions around the world will get breast cancer. I have seen far too many women (and their families) have to deal with this trauma, and my goal in writing this book is to make sure this doesn't happen to you. Breast cancer is not inevitable; you don't have to just sit and wait to get it. By taking small, easy, and inexpensive steps now, you may avoid catastrophe in the future and skip that personal "terrorist" we call breast cancer. As you will see, it's never too late to start and never too early to begin. Make sure you read this book and then share the information with your daughter, sister, mother, or friend. It will be the greatest gift you could possibly give them—the gift of health and perhaps the gift of life!

So where do we begin? Let's start by clearing up a misconception that everyone who gets breast cancer has a genetic predisposition. Then we will discuss estrogen: how it works, the role it plays in breast cancer, and why millions of women have been taking the most dangerous type of estrogen to relieve their symptoms. We will talk about tests that may save your life, and then I will share with you 20 "secrets" that may lower your breast cancer risk by 90 percent or more. So let's get started with a brief discussion about genes.

Assess Your Genetic Risk

Many people have an incorrect understanding of genetics. There is the prevailing belief that if a woman has the genes for breast cancer, she will get breast cancer—it is predetermined. In addition, many people believe that everyone who gets breast cancer has a genetic predisposition for it. But in reality, only a minority of women who get breast cancer have a true genetic predisposition for it. The majority of women who get breast cancer do not have a genetic predisposition.

In fact, there was a wonderful study that sheds light on the genetic versus environment debate. This study, published in the *New England Journal of Medicine* in 2000, showed that only approximately 27 percent of breast cancer is genetic. This means that 73 percent of those studied had no genetic predisposition for breast cancer.[1] Researchers looked at 44,788 pairs of twins from Scandinavia to evaluate their risk of breast cancer. The results found that 27 percent of the women who were the twin of a woman with breast cancer actually got breast cancer. This, of course, means that 73 percent of the twin sisters did *not* get breast cancer. If breast cancer is genetically predetermined, why didn't all of the twin sisters of those women with breast cancer also get breast cancer?

The answer is easy: breast cancer is not entirely genetically pre-determined. The women who did not get breast cancer clearly did something different than their sisters that allowed them to avoid it. So what did they do? This we do not know, since the study did not evaluate the noncancer twin to see what variables were different, such as diet and other lifestyle factors. The conclusion of the study was as follows: "Inherited genetic factors make a *minor* contribution to susceptibility to most types of neoplasms (cancer). This finding indicates the environment has the principal role in causing sporadic cancer." If environmental factors play a major role in causing breast cancer, then why don't we find out what these factors are so that we can avoid them and reduce our risk? The answer, to a great extent, is that we already know what these factors are! The problem is that there is not a lot of money to be made in keeping you from getting breast cancer. In fact, you will see that many of the changes you can make to reduce your risk are extremely inexpensive.

Because many of the supplements that you can take to reduce your risk cannot be patented, major pharmaceutical companies are not interested in them. (Without a patent, there is no money to be made.) And our government has done little research on these supplements because it is so closely tied to the pharmaceutical industry. In addition, there is a bias in the medical community against natural/nutritional preventive medicine. As we talked about in the Introduction, doctors are used to fighting a "war" on breast cancer after you have it. Most of you would be shocked to learn how little training a physician receives in how to keep you from becoming ill or getting cancer in the first place.

Lastly, there seems to be a general misconception that the causes of cancer are just too intricate for us to know. If the causes are not known, then there is nothing you can do about it—except sit and wait. As you will see throughout this book, that is a fallacy. I do not pretend to know every cause of breast cancer. Certainly, significant information will be discovered over the next decade that we do not know now. However, a large amount of research has already been conducted. Very compelling studies have been completed that show simple steps you can take to reduce your risk of breast cancer.

Before we go on to the environmental factors, let's take some time to talk about genetic factors, since many of you have close relatives who have had breast cancer. Everyone will hear more and more about the genetic tests available that can evaluate if you have a genetic predisposition. Many of you will wonder if you should have these tests done. Furthermore, if the tests are positive, is there anything you can do about it? Let's start with what genetic tests are available and what they tell you.

BRCA1 AND BRCA2

BRCA1 and BRCA2 are tumor suppressor genes, which help with DNA repair. There are several other tumor suppressor genes that are currently under investigation, but these are the two genes whose mutations are most closely associated with an increased genetic risk of breast cancer. Some women inherit mutations of these two genes. These inherited mutations are responsible for a minority of breast cancer—only about 7 to 10 percent of all breast cancers. Yet, if you do have one of these genetic mutations, your risk of breast cancer is significantly higher. If you have a BRCA mutation and you are over the age of 50, your risk is 33 to 50 percent (significantly higher than in the general population). By the time you turn 70, your risk increases to 55 to 80 percent. (If you have this genetic mutation, you also have a 28 to 44 percent risk of developing ovarian cancer by age 70 to 80.)[2]

How does this work? You have two copies of all your genes, including BRCA1 and BRCA2.If you were born with "normal" BRCA genes, you would need to damage both copies of BRCA1 or BRCA2 to get mutations in both copies. Women with inherited mutations are born with a mutation to one copy of BRCA1 or BRCA2. This means that they only need to damage the other (normal) copy to cause a mutation. Damaging one copy of the gene, of course, is much easier than damaging two copies. Consider this analogy: If you're driving with two tires on each wheel and you have a flat or blowout on one tire, you still have one intact tire and can continue to drive. But if you have only one tire on each wheel, a blowout of that tire causes significant instability.

Women from the general population have about a one-fourth of 1 percent (0.25 percent) chance of having a BRCA1 mutation. Certain ethnic groups—like Ashkenazi Jews, for example—have a significantly higher chance.

How do you know if you have a BRCA1 or BRCA2 mutation? Testing is available through oncologists, genetic clinics, and hospitals.

Who Should Be Tested?

Here are some characteristics seen in families with hereditary cancer syndromes:

- Several relatives with breast cancer and/or ovarian cancer
- Unusually young age of onset of the cancers
- Two or more primary cancers in the same person. (Primary means that they are not metastasized from another cancer. In other words, the cancers are completely unrelated to one another.)
- Cancers in both breasts and/or in both ovaries
- Family history associated with other diseases that are directly inherited[3]

If you have several relatives who have had breast cancer, particularly if the cancer occurred younger than age 50, and/or family members with cancer in both breasts or ovaries, you should consider getting tested for an inherited BRCA1 or BRCA2 mutation.

What Can Be Done If You Have a Genetic BRCA1/BRCA2 Abnormality?

- Keep very close surveillance. If you have only one intact copy of BRCA1 or BRCA2, then you need much closer monitoring and at a younger age than a woman who does not have the mutation.
- Consider taking tamoxifen or raloxifene. These two drugs, which are used to treat breast cancer, may also play a role in preventing it. One study has shown that in women with BRCA mutations who have been diagnosed with breast cancer, tamoxifen reduced the risk of developing cancer in

the other breast by 75 percent. The tamoxifen was used for 2 to 4 years. (See our discussion of tamoxifen and ralox-ifene in Step 18 for more information about these drugs and their associated side effects.)[4]

- Consider prophylactic bilateral mastectomy and/or oophorectomy (removal of both breasts and/or ovaries). Prophylactic mastectomy reduces the risk of breast cancer by 90 percent in women with a family history and other significant risk factors. This is a recommendation that I personally disagree with, but it is still an option for those of you at very high risk. In my opinion, the recommendation to remove both breasts prophylactically is comparable to the Civil War days, when a soldier with a wounded toe had his leg removed to prevent gangrene.

We are here to give you information on how to avoid breast cancer while keeping your breasts. So, what can be done if you are part of the small percentage of women with BRCA mutations? You must do everything you can to protect your one normal copy of BRCA1 and/or BRCA2. This may include taking the following supplements: (1) I3C and/or DIM, (2) folate and B_{12}, (3) curcumin, and (4) green tea phenols.

We will discuss all of these nutrients in great detail in later steps. I think you will find this information extraordinary, since one study shows that these nutrients can protect BRCA genes from becoming damaged. This is vital groundbreaking research for those of you with BRCA mutations. For the rest of you who were not born with inherited mutations, you want to do everything possible to protect your two copies of BRCA1 and BRCA2 tumor suppressor genes. Following the plan outlined in later steps of this book will help you do just that. We will also discuss how those of you with two intact BRCA genes can damage both of them through free radical oxidative damage, thereby causing breast cancer. More importantly, we will discuss how you can prevent that damage from happening.

Now that we have briefly reviewed the genetic factors involved, we need to discuss estrogen—the role it plays in causing breast cancer and the steps you can take to prevent estrogen from harming your breasts.

ESTROGEN

Despite all of the press surrounding the 2002 study on estrogen, estrogen alone does not cause breast cancer; if it did, every 18-year-old female would have cancer. Breast cancer involves a complex process; many factors combine to cause the disease we call breast cancer. Remember the movie *The Perfect Storm*, where three storms all converged to create one giant, overwhelming storm? Breast cancer is like that: you must have several factors all coming together over a number of years to create the disease. As we've seen, genetic damage plays a part, because without genetic damage, breast cancer cannot develop. Estrogen has an important role, since it is responsible for breast cell stimulation. In general, the more stimulation your breast cells receive, the more those cells with damaged DNA can overreproduce, resulting in breast cancer. Estrogen's role depends on several important factors:

- What type of estrogen you make (or take) and in what quantity

- How you detoxify your estrogen and to what metabolites (some of which increase breast cancer risk)
- If you take the type of estrogen replacement that increases your risk, and how long you have been taking it
- If you are deficient in the important antioxidants necessary to detoxify estrogen and protect your breasts from genetic damage
- How much exposure you get to the everyday chemicals that increase breast cancer risk

THE BOTTOM LINE

Breast cancer is complicated. It depends on the amount of genetic damage sometimes inherited but more often developed throughout your life; how much estrogen you take and/or make; what type of estrogen and how you detoxify that estrogen. And it depends on how well (or how poorly) you protect your breast genes from damage throughout your life. We will review all of these factors in the next few steps, and I think you will be amazed at how easy it is to make small changes in your diet and lifestyle that may make big changes in your breast cancer risk. Let's move on now and discuss the whole estrogen controversy, including how the estrogen you take may be the most dangerous!

Know Your
Estrogen Quotient

Estrogen alone does not cause breast cancer. Breast cancer is a complex process in which many factors combine to cause the disease. As we've seen, genetic predisposition plays a part, although that role has been greatly exaggerated. Environmental factors play the greatest role in the causation of all cancer, particularly breast cancer. In Step 1, we discussed genetic predisposition versus environmental factors. It is important to remember that the development of breast cancer depends on several important factors:

- How much and what type of estrogen do you make?
- Are you detoxifying estrogen to the more dangerous metabolites, which increase your risk of breast cancer?
- Are you taking the type of estrogen supplement that increases your breast cancer risk, and how long have you been taking that supplement?
- Are you low in the essential nutrients necessary to metabolize estrogen to the "good metabolite"?
- Do you lack the important antioxidants that are vital in repairing and protecting the DNA in your breast tissue?

• Have you been exposed to the chemicals that mimic estrogen and cause your breast cells to reproduce wildly? (Nearly all American women have traces of these chemicals in their breast milk).

So you see, breast cancer is a far more complex issue than the relatively simple question, Does estrogen cause breast cancer? The answer to that question depends to a great degree on how you answer the other questions. We will review each one of these factors in detail throughout this book. You will learn how to alter each one of these risk factors so that they can begin to work in your favor.

Let's take some time to talk about estrogen. There is so much information and misinformation concerning estrogen that it can become confusing. We will begin talking about the different types of estrogen (estrogen is not one hormone, but multiple hormones) and which estrogens contribute to breast cancer and which estrogen may actually protect against breast cancer.

WHY TAKE ESTROGEN IN THE FIRST PLACE?

Fourteen million women in the United States are on supplemental estrogen replacement therapy (ERT). In addition, millions of women throughout the world take estrogen replacement therapy to control estrogen deficiency symptoms caused by either natural or surgical menopause. Symptoms of estrogen deficiency include:

• *Classical menopausal symptoms.* Typical symptoms may include hot flashes, vaginal dryness, night sweats, sleep

disturbances, depression, reduced libido, loss of enjoy-
ment of sex, and increased urinary incontinence.
- *Cognitive decline.* Symptoms may include difficulty with
  short-term memory and trouble processing information.
- *Osteoporosis.* Estrogen replacement reduces the risk of
  osteoporosis by as much as 30 to 60 percent.
- *Heart disease.* The data are more controversial concerning ERT's ability to reduce the risk of heart disease.
  Some studies in the past showed a reduction of heart
  disease for women taking ERT. More recent studies,
  however, have questioned that conclusion. The type of
  estrogen and the dose given could make a significant
  difference in the reduction of heart disease. Estrogen
  traditionally has been thought to be the reason why
  women have a lower risk of heart attack up to menopause. After menopause, a woman's risk increases rapidly, and after a few years it approaches the risk seen for
  men. Almost all of the studies on heart disease have
  used the strong estrogens (estrone and estradiol) for
  their estrogen replacement. As we will see in the next
  step, it may not be the strong estrogens that confer the
  protective effect, but a different hormone or a combination of hormones.

Depending on the individual, the decrease of estrogen at menopause can range from irritating to devastating. Vaginal dryness and
lack of lubrication can be frustrating, for example, but can usually
be helped with a water-based lubricant. For other women, this problem can become severe to the point that intercourse becomes intol-
erable. Many women also develop sleep disturbances, depression,

fatigue, and memory disturbances, all of which can be devastating to their ability to function on a day-to-day basis. The importance of a good night's sleep cannot be overemphasized. For many women, the problem is twofold, for they will experience a decreased amount of sleep as a result of hot flashes, night sweats, and other neurological factors. These women may also suffer from a decreased quality of sleep. Lack of estrogen significantly decreases your sleep quality along with quantity. So for millions of women, this is not just about putting up with some symptoms but is a major problem that significantly reduces their quality of life and in many cases reduces their ability to function both at work and at home.

THE THREE MAJOR TYPES OF ESTROGEN

Most women think of estrogen as a single hormone, when in reality it is three separate hormones: estradiol (E2), estrone (E1), and estriol (E3).

Estradiol (E2)

Estradiol (E2) is the most commonly prescribed estrogen replacement. This includes conjugated estrogen, since it is converted to 17 beta-estradiol in the body. These conjugated estrogens were one of the first supplemental estrogens developed for commercial use during the twentieth century. They are made by collecting the urine from pregnant horses (mares) and refining that urine to collect the estrogen. (Estrogen is not made by plants, only animals.) Although it would seem that conjugated estrogens might be safer than synthetic estrogen, since they are from a "natural" source, this form of replacement has several potential problems:

- Conjugated estrogens are converted to 17 beta-estradiol in the body. 17 beta-estradiol goes into the estrogen quotient as estradiol and therefore lowers your estrogen quotient and increases your breast cancer risk. The higher the dose of conjugated estrogens you take, the lower your estrogen quotient (EQ).
- 17 beta-estradiol may be predominantly converted by your liver to the 16 OH metabolite. (A metabolite is a by-product of metabolism.) As we will discuss in Step 5, 16 OH metabolites are associated with increased risk of breast cancer. The higher your level of 16 OH metabolites, the higher your risk of breast cancer.
- There are estrogens in conjugated estrogen that horses need but women may not need (horse estrogen is obviously meant for horses).
- Conjugated estrogens are usually prescribed in pill form. Therefore, they have a major problem associated with them, called the first-pass effect.

The First-Pass Effect. Estrogen supplements taken in pill form are absorbed through the digestive tract first and sent to the liver to be metabolized. Up to 90 percent of the estrogen pill can be metabolized by your liver into the 16 OH metabolite prior to being released to your bloodstream for delivery to your tissues. It is the 16 OH metabolite that your breast tissue receives. As we will discuss in Step 4, the 16 OH metabolite has been associated with an increased risk of breast cancer. The lower your 16 OH metabolite level, the lower your risk of breast cancer. So the question is: Why in the world would you want to take an estrogen that lowers your EQ and is converted predominantly to the 16 OH metabolite, which is associated with increased breast cancer risk?

How Can You Avoid the First-Pass Effect? Transdermal (through the skin) estrogen is available by patch or cream. Estrogen placed on the skin goes directly into the bloodstream and is delivered to your breasts before it goes to the liver. This means that your breasts actually "see" the estrogen supplement first, not the 16 OH metabolite. It is estrogen that binds to the estrogen receptors (ERs) in your breasts, not the 16 OH metabolite. That's the good news.

The bad news is that most estrogen patches or creams are the strong form of estrogen, either estradiol or conjugated estrogens. This means that they will still lower your EQ and increase your risk of breast cancer. Even though you have avoided the first-pass effect, the strong estrogens lower your EQ and eventually metabolize predominantly to the 16 OH metabolite. Both of these factors will increase your risk of breast cancer. (There is a safer estrogen cream, which we will discuss in Step 3.)

There is another problem with estrogen pills. Estrogen pills (tablets) release their medicine unevenly. When you take a tablet, the level of estrogen in your blood rises in the first few hours and then lowers later in the day. Symptoms often return after a few hours, so you must take another tablet or a stronger dose the first time. This causes you to take a dose higher than you might ordinarily need if you were using a cream or patch. A cream releases more slowly, using your skin as a slow-release mechanism. (The patch uses a slow-release barrier.) A cream or patch gives you a slower, steadier release of medication plus better absorption. This allows you to use a lower dose than you would have to use with oral medication.

Estrone (E1)

Estrone (E1) is converted in the body primarily to the 16 OH metabolite. Moreover, estrone is usually given via pill. Therefore, it has all of the problems associated with strong oral estrogen replacement that we have discussed. Estrone has been linked with an increased risk of breast cancer. The exact mechanism of this is unknown, although we already know that taking estrone lowers your EQ, which, in turn increases your risk of developing breast cancer. And as we have just said, estrone is predominantly converted to the 16 OH metabolite, another risk factor. These are two possible explanations why estrone can increase your overall risk of breast cancer.

Estriol (E3)

Finally, there is an estrogen replacement named estriol (E3) that is not converted to the 16 OH metabolite and therefore does not lower your EMI. It increases your EQ by definition, therefore reducing your risk of breast cancer. It can be given topically by cream, avoiding the first-pass effect and using your skin as a slow-release mechanism to obtain steady blood levels throughout the day. The question is, Does this form of estrogen control the symptoms associated with menopause, and if so, where has it been, and why don't more doctors know about it? To answer this question, see Step 3, where we discuss estriol—what it is and why it is the "safest estrogen."

Most of you have never heard of estriol, although it is the type of estrogen that is highest in your body. In fact, a recent study has shown that estriol is significantly higher than the sum of estrone and estradiol.[1] Estrone and estradiol are the "strongest" estrogens you make. This means that you produce them in lower amounts, and they fluctuate more significantly than estriol. Doctors have prescribed these strong estrogens as supplements for nearly fifty years. Most doctors have mistakenly thought that since estriol is weaker, it is too weak to be effective as replacement therapy. They believed that since estrone and estradiol are stronger and relieve menopausal symptoms in lower dosages, they are the best estrogens to give for menopausal replacement. It now appears that this is an incorrect assumption! Estriol, the weaker estrogen, is naturally high in a woman's body for a reason: it protects your breasts from overstimulation and overproduction of breast cells. By giving women estrone and estradiol as supplements, doctors have been decreasing the estrogen quotient (EQ) for millions of women for half a century. The EQ is equal to the amount of estriol divided by estrone plus estradiol.

$$EQ = \frac{Estriol}{Estrone + Estradiol}$$

Your EQ is one of the best predictors of your risk of breast cancer.[2] The vast majority of American women do not know their EQ. Even worse, their doctors don't know about the importance of this level. The test for EQ is an easy, relatively inexpensive urine test that may predict, years in advance, if you are going to get breast cancer.

Therefore, this test may save your life. Most importantly, if your EQ is low, you can take steps now to improve it and reduce your chance of getting breast cancer. In my opinion, every woman should know her EQ, especially if she is starting ERT or has a family history of breast cancer! As you can see from the equation on the previous page, when you take supplemental estradiol or estrone without getting increased amounts of estriol, by definition you are lowering your EQ and increasing your risk of breast cancer. Even worse, if you are menopausal or postmenopausal, then you are making less estriol than when you were premenopausal; therefore, your estriol is lower (in the case of surgical menopause, very low) at the same time that you are taking supplemental estrone or estradiol. This reduces your estrogen quotient dramatically. *This is a recipe for increasing your risk of breast cancer!* Doctors have unknowingly been helping to create lower estrogen quotients and therefore increasing the risk of breast cancer through the very medicines they have been prescribing to control postmenopausal symptoms.

To compound this problem, doctors have been prescribing these strong estrogens in the worst possible form: pills. Oral estrone and estradiol are the most commonly prescribed ERT in the world. In the year 2000, nearly 70 million prescriptions were written in the United States for Premarin and/or Prempro alone.[3] (Premarin and Prempro are brand names of conjugated estrogen or conjugated estrogen with synthetic progestins). In the next step, we'll find out more about estriol, the safest form of estrogen.

Learn About Estriol (E3): The Safer Estrogen

So much confusion concerning estrogen was created by the woman's health study. In the media, estrogen is talked about as if it is one hormone, yet as we discussed in Step 2 it is actually three. In addition, estrogen is now considered "bad," yet as you will see there is a type of estrogen that is safer and may actually protect your breasts from the over-stimulation that contributes to breast cancer.

WHAT IS ESTRIOL (E3)?

Estriol is the weakest of the three major estrogens you make. Like the other two estrogens, estrone (E1) and estradiol (E2), it is made from cholesterol via several steps.[1] It has recently been shown that you make more estriol than the other two estrogens combined.[2] Estriol is highest when you are pregnant and appears to have a protective effect on both fetus and mother. After delivery, estriol appears to have a protective effect on the breasts, and women who have been pregnant have more estriol, which appears to be the reason why women who have had multiple pregnancies are at a lower risk for breast cancer than women who have never been pregnant. Similarly, research has shown that women who had their first baby at a young age are at a reduced risk for breast cancer. These women have higher estriol levels at an earlier age and maintain higher levels for the rest of their lives. The fact that they have enjoyed estriol's protective effect for a longer period of time may be the reason for their lower risk of breast cancer.

WHY IS ESTRIOL PROTECTIVE OF BREAST TISSUE?

Estriol is not converted to the 16 OH or 4 OH metabolite. As we will see in Step 4, high levels of the 16 OH or 4 OH metabolite *increase* your risk of breast cancer. The stronger estrogens, estrone and estradiol, can be—and often are—converted to the 16 OH or 4 OH metabolite.

Estriol does not lower your estrogen quotient (we discussed the importance of estrogen quotient in Step 2). When you use estrone or estradiol as a supplement, you lower your estrogen quotient and by definition increase your risk of breast cancer.

Although estriol is a weak estrogen, it is able to attach to your estrogen receptors (ERs). If estriol is attached to the estrogen receptors in your breasts, the stronger estrogens like estradiol and/or the 16 OH metabolite *can't* bind. If the strong estrogens can't bind, they cannot overstimulate your breast tissue and therefore can't increase your risk of getting breast cancer. Studies done on mice show that estriol reduces the breast-stimulating effects of estradiol.[3]

Another study showed that not only did intermittent estriol treatment not increase breast cancer, but it "demonstrated the most significant antimammary carcinogenic activity of twenty-two tested compounds in rats that were fed two known carcinogens."[4]

WHAT DO THE STUDIES TELL US?

Remember the estrogen quotient (EQ) discussed in the last step? Your EQ is the amount of estriol in your body divided by the sum of the estrone and estradiol. A study of 26 women with breast cancer showed a median EQ of 0.5 before menopause and 0.8 after menopause. This was compared with healthy women in the study who had ratios of 1.3 before menopause and 1.2 after menopause.[5] This study showed that women with breast cancer had lower EQs than women who were healthy. Premenopausal women with breast cancer had EQs less than half that of the healthy women. Postmenopausal women with breast cancer had EQs 44 percent lower than healthy postmenopausal women. To have a lower EQ, by definition, you must either have less estriol or more estrone and/or estradiol.

We know from the study that the women with breast cancer had 30 to 60 percent *less* estriol than the women without cancer. According to the findings of this study, the women with the higher estriol levels, and therefore higher EQ levels, were at a *significantly reduced* risk of breast cancer. Why is this study and others like it so important? As you will see, estriol is effective in reducing and/or controlling many of the symptoms of menopause, including hot flashes, night sweats, vaginal atrophy, skin aging, cognitive decline, and possibly bone loss, yet it increases the EQ, which by definition may *lower* your breast cancer risk.

Moreover, estriol does not seem to promote excessive uterine lining buildup or blood clots. Is there really an estrogen that will control your menopausal symptoms but not increase your breast cancer risk and may actually decrease your risk? Let's take a look at several studies that may answer this question.

ESTRIOL AND MENOPAUSAL SYMPTOMS

The evidence is fairly clear that for most women, estriol can control their menopausal symptoms. The only question is, at what dosage?

- *Study 1.* This study used 2 to 8 milligrams of estriol per day (by mouth) on a group of 52 postmenopausal women who were having significant menopausal symptoms. The estriol was used for 6 months, and significant improvement was seen in hot flashes, insomnia, depression, arthralgia (joint pain), headache, palpitations, dyspareunia (painful sex), vaginal dryness, and loss of libido. The most significant improvement occurred in the group that received 8 milligrams a day, yet improvement was seen at even 2 milligrams per day. (Remember, this estriol was given orally. Oral estriol is not well absorbed and may be the reason why high doses of estriol were needed to control symptoms. If the estriol had been given topically—through the skin—a smaller dose could have been used, since topical estriol is better absorbed.) Of great importance is that no significant side effects were noted in any group in this study. Pap smears all remained normal. Mammograms done on six women with fibrocystic breasts showed no changes. Blood pressure and weight stayed normal. Spotting occurred in only two women, but lasted for only 2 to 3 days and then stopped despite continued medication. Endometrial biopsies of these two women were normal. No blood clots or cardiovascular side effects were noted.[6]

- *Study 2.* This study involved 20 postmenopausal women, ages 44 to 62. The women were given 2 milligrams of estriol (pills) for 2 years. The authors concluded that these women had "improvement of major subjective climacteric [menopausal complaints] in 86 percent of patients, especially hot flashes and insomnia, within 3 months. The atrophic genital changes (changes in the vagina's appearance and feel) caused by estrogen deficiency were improved satisfactorily. No side effects of the therapy were noted. Only one patient had uterine bleeding"[7] This study did not show, however, that estriol could prevent osteoporosis, a common benefit of standard estrogen replacement therapy (ERT). This study showed that menopausal symptoms were well controlled with a moderate dose of estriol and that no side effects were seen when monitored over a fairly substantial period of time addressing key questions concerning estriol treatment of menopausal symptoms: Can we use a low dose and is it safe?
- *Study 3.* One hundred fifty postmenopausal women were given 1 milligram of estriol for 2 years. These women showed a significant improvement in their menopausal symptoms. On average, the Kupperman index dropped from 34 before estriol to 6 after 3 months on estriol.[8] As you can see from Table 3.1, a drop in the Kupperman index from an average of 34 to an average of 6 is a significant improvement in quality of life. This change occurred on a relatively small dose of oral estriol. (This is comparable to a much lower dose of topical estriol, possibly 0.5 to 1 milligram or less per day.)

Table 3.1 Kupperman Index

Symptoms *"Major"*	Symptoms *"Minor"*
Hot flashes	Nervousness
Insomnia	Dizziness
Headache	Joint pain
Excessive sweating	Tremor
Depression	Tachycardia
	Irritability
	Lack of concentration

Scale: 0 = absent
1 = present (low)
2 = moderate
3 = severe
4 = very severe

Note: Scores of "major" symptoms are doubled.

Source: H. S. Kupperman et al., *JAMA* (1959), 171:1627.

Discussion

These three studies show that estriol provided women significant relief of their menopausal symptoms without major side effects. It is important to note that an oral dose as low as 1 milligram gave significant relief, improving menopausal symptoms within 90 days, and no side effects were noted over the course of 2 years. This shows that even at low doses, estriol can reduce menopausal symptoms with low risk of significant side effects.

ESTRIOL AND YOUR UTERUS

Many medical studies have shown that the strong estrogens —
estrone, estradiol, and conjugated estrogens—increases a woman's
risk for endometrial cancer (cancer of the lining of the uterus)
if taken without progesterone. Does estriol cause problems with
overproduction of the lining of the uterus? (Overproduction can
lead to endometrial cancer.) Let's take a look at four medical studies evaluating the safety of estriol.

- *Study 1.* A study looking at twelve different studies
  involving 214 women who used estriol vaginal cream
  showed all endometrial biopsies normal for age. Biopsies were done from 6 months to 2 years after starting
  estriol. The conclusion of this study was that "single
  daily treatment with intravaginal estriol in the recommended dose in postmenopausal women is safe and
  without an increased risk of endometrial proliferation
  (when endometrial tissue begins to overgrow in the
  uterus) or hyperplasia" (an increase in the number of
  cells inside the uterus).[8]
- *Study 2.* A study published in the *Journal of the American Medical Association* found no endometrial changes
  in 52 women given up to 8 milligrams of estriol per day
  for 6 months. The authors of the study concluded, "This
  agent's [estriol's] capacity to relieve vasomotor instability [hot flashes and night sweats] and improve vaginal
  maturation without notable side effects is sufficient
  reason to include this drug in the management of postmenopausal symptoms."[9]

- *Study 3.* A study published in the *European Journal of Obstetrics and Gynecology* found that 8 milligrams of estriol once per day caused slight endometrial changes, as compared with 4 milligrams twice a day, which caused greater endometrial changes.[10] (This is surprising, because generally a lower dose of medication given more frequently is safer and associated with fewer side effects than a higher dose given less often. Something to consider is that 8 milligrams a day is a high dose of estriol, and perhaps 4 milligrams twice per day was absorbed better and therefore delivered significantly more estriol to the uterus than the 8 milligrams once per day. This is author's speculation, however, since no definite mechanism was determined in this study.)
- *Study 4.* Estriol was given to 48 women who were scheduled for hysterectomy. The dose was 1 milligram twice daily for 10 to 25 days. As many as 71 percent of these women showed endometrial hyperplastic changes (the lining of the uterus was growing). It should be noted that 22 of these women also received a stronger conjugated estrogen by vaginal suppository.[11] This study shows that in some cases, estriol may increase the uterine lining. Therefore, despite the fact that the majority of studies did not show any lining increase, we cannot say that it is impossible for estriol to increase uterine cancer risk.

Discussion

So what does all of this mean?

- In most studies, estriol did not cause excessive growth of the uterine lining. In some women, it may cause excessive growth if given in a large dose over a long period of time. Remember, you are a unique individual with unique biochemical responses to any medication or supplement.
- It appears to be safer to use the smallest amount of estriol as infrequently as possible to control menopausal symptoms. Once per day appears better than twice per day. Every other day appears safer than daily. Therefore, you should use the least amount of estriol necessary to control your symptoms.
- As we will discuss in Step 8, we almost always use bioidentical progesterone cream in combination with estriol. This means that rarely will estriol be unopposed. This should make the uterine cancer issue a mute point, since progesterone should protect your uterine lining from overproduction and therefore prevent the small likelihood of uterine lining overgrowth with estriol.

ESTRIOL AND YOUR BONES

One of the major "drawbacks" of estriol has been that most physicians concluded that it does not protect you from osteoporosis. This is one of the reasons that the stronger estrogens won the confidence of American physicians and became one of the most widely prescribed medications in the United States. The other reason, of course, is money. The stronger estrogens could be patented and become the property of pharmaceutical corporations. Estriol, because it is bioidentical, could not be patented and therefore was not promoted.

Is the "Knock" on Estriol Justified?
Does It Protect You from Osteoporosis?

Let's look at the scientific studies.

- *Study 1.* A study in Japan showed an increase in bone mineral density (BMD) after 2 milligrams a day of estriol plus 800 milligrams of calcium lactate for almost a year. BMD increased almost 2 percent.[12]
- *Study 2.* According to another Japanese study, a small group of women given 2 milligrams of estradiol a day, plus 2,000 milligrams of calcium lactate a day, showed an improvement in bone mineral density of 1.7 percent versus a control group that received the calcium only. The control group actually had a decrease in BMD after 52 weeks. In addition, the estriol group had a decrease in all measures of bone destruction compared with the control group.[13]
- *Study 3.* In a third Japanese study, 18 women given estriol plus calcium lactate (2 milligrams a day of estriol plus 1 gram a day of calcium lactate) showed an increase in

BMD of 5.6 percent, with the women who just received
calcium losing bone density by 4 percent.[14]

- *Study 4.* A study from the *Chinese Medical Journal* indicated that estriol was a very effective treatment for postmenopausal symptoms but did not prevent
osteoporosis.[15]

- *Study 5.* This study showed that intravaginal estriol given
to 214 healthy, postmenopausal women reduced the
decrease in BMD seen in the control group, which was
given calcium only. Estriol slowed, but did not totally
prevent, the drop in BMD seen with the control group.
When salmon calcitonin was added to estriol plus calcium, there was a significant improvement in BMD,
along with control of postmenopausal symptoms.[16]
(Salmon calcitonin is a medication given by injection or
nasal spray as a treatment for osteopeniaor osteoporosis.
It is generally well tolerated and has few side effects; the
only contraindication being that you cannot take this
medication if you are allergic to salmon.)

Discussion

Does estriol protect your bones from osteoporosis? Some studies
say it does and others disagree. We all agree that osteoporosis is a
very serious disease that kills thousands of women per year in the
United States (including my mother). It is vital that your bones
be protected. We have seen that estriol controls menopausal symptoms with very few side effects and that it may protect bone, even

without the addition of other medications. If we assume that it does not, then you can very easily maintain your bone strength by exercise, calcium supplementation, phytonutrients, natural progesterone, and/or the addition of salmon calcitonin or other medications. You can use any combination of the above to maintain your BMD. Monitor your bone density yearly by dual photon densitometry and urinary bone breakdown products. If breakdown products are high in your urine, you are losing bone.

ESTRIOL AND VAGINAL/URINARY COMPLAINTS

So far, we have learned that estriol controls menopausal symptoms without apparent serious side effects and that it does not appear to stimulate overgrowth of the uterine lining. The evidence is less certain about protecting you from bone loss, but even if it doesn't, your bone strength can be maintained with the addition of salmon calcitonin and/or progesterone, both of which are very safe and well tolerated. But does estriol improve vaginal function and/or poor urinary control, problems often associated with postmenopausal loss of estrogen? Let's look at four studies.

- *Study 1.* Estriol was given to 263 menopausal women, with half of them receiving 2 to 4 milligrams per *week*. This study showed that even this low dose of estriol was able to restore normal vaginal function without causing excessive uterine endometrial growth.[17]
- *Study 2.* In this study, 41 women with severe atrophic vaginitis received low-dose estriol at 0.5 milligram per

day. Atrophic vaginitis is dysfunction of the vagina caused by lack of estrogen. Without estrogen, the lining of the vagina loses its stretchability and often becomes inflamed, red, and painful. Urethral cells are the cells of the tube that carries urine from the bladder to the outside. Without estrogen, these cells can become damaged and/or distressed, causing loss of urinary control, burning, and/or frequency of urination. Happily, estriol restored vaginal function and normal urethral cells with 2 weeks of therapy.[18]

- *Study 3.* In this study, 3.5 milligrams of estriol was given vaginally for 3 months to 135 postmenopausal women with inability to hold their urine. On this regimen, *over 60 percent* of the women saw an improvement with their incontinence. Painful urination improved in *all* of the estriol groups. The frequency with which the women urinated dropped significantly.[19]

- *Study 4.* Estriol was shown to improve good bacteria in the vagina and reduce urinary tract infections. This study concluded that "intravaginal estriol was associated with a significant decrease in vaginal pH."[20]

Discussion

In the case studies above, estriol helped lower the pH of the vagina to a more healthy acidity, allowing better growth of good bacteria and slowing the growth of bad bacteria. If the vagina stays clear of bad bacteria, there will be fewer urinary tract infections (UTIs). The fewer UTIs you have, the less antibiotics you need. The less antibiotics, the less damage to the good bacteria in your vagina and the less likelihood that you will develop vaginal yeast. One of the first things most of you have discovered when you take an antibiotic is that you develop vaginal yeast. The reason for this is that the antibiotic kills many of the good bacteria in your vagina, but does not kill yeast or certain bad bacteria. This allows those bad bacteria or yeast to overgrow and cause an infection. In addition, estriol directly improved vaginal function and urethral cellular health.

Therefore, women in these studies had less pain with intercourse, fewer vaginal infections, less frequency of urination, fewer UTIs, and better sexual function.

ESTRIOL AND YOUR SKIN

Most postmenopausal women complain of sagging skin—increasing wrinkles and drooping skin of the neck, arms, buttocks, belly, and breasts. Estrogen plays a key role in maintaining the elastin fibers in your skin. As your estrogen level drops, the skin loses its elasticity, and your skin wrinkles and sags. The result of estrogen on skin is dramatic.

I have seen old wrinkled men who were placed on estrogen (as a treatment for prostate cancer) develop the skin of a 30-year-old in a matter of months.

It is fairly well documented that strong ERT can improve your skin's elasticity, but it also increases your risk of breast cancer. What about estriol? Can it help your skin? We've already seen that the risk of developing breast cancer from estriol appears to be low.

Let's look at a couple of interesting studies that review estriol's effect on your skin.

- *Study 1.* This study showed that 1 milligram of estriol applied topically once daily improved the elastin in 50 percent of the women treated after only 3 weeks. None of the control group improved.[21]
- *Study 2.* From the *International Journal of Dermatology*, this study compared 0.3 percent estriol cream to 0.01 percent estradiol cream applied to the face and neck for 3 months. Both groups consisted of postmenopausal women who were not on other hormone replacement therapy. The conclusion was: "Both types of estrogen markedly improved elasticity and firmness of the skin and reduced wrinkle depth and pore size dramatically, by approximately 61 to 100 percent. In addition, skin moisture improved and no systemic hormonal side effects were noted."[22]

Discussion

Both of these studies showed that estriol can help aging skin by improving elastin, collagen, and moisture of the skin. It should be noted that in both of these studies, estriol was applied directly to the skin that was measured. It is unknown how much systemic estriol will help the face when it is applied elsewhere. My clinical judgment would be that you should see some improvement or better maintenance of your skin tone, but perhaps not as much improvement as the 61 to 100 percent that was achieved by direct application of the estriol to the face.

ESTRIOL AND CHOLESTEROL,
BLOOD PRESSURE, AND BLOOD CLOTS

Past studies have suggested that traditional ERT (estrone and/or estradiol) provided some cardiac protective effect for women. Premenopausal women are at a significantly reduced risk for coronary artery disease (plugging of the heart arteries) compared with men their age. The explanation for this has always been that estrogen is the protective agent.

Women on average have higher levels of "good cholesterol" (high-density lipoprotein, or HDL) compared with men their age. HDL has a protective effect on the arteries. After menopause, cardiac lipids change, and a woman's cardiac risk climbs quickly; within several years after menopause, she is at nearly the same risk as a man her age. Recently, the Women's Health Initiative (WHI) showed that conjugated estrogen plus synthetic progestin actually increased cardiac risk!

This is the study that caused so much controversy in the summer of 2002. The study was stopped because of the unacceptable increase in risk of breast cancer for those women on conjugated estrogen plus synthetic progestin. However, the levels of increasing cardiac risk were nearly approaching the point where the study would be stopped for those reasons as well.

What do the studies tell us concerning estriol? Does it control coronary risk factors, blood pressure, and/or blood clots? Let's look at a few of the studies.

- **Study 1.** A study in the *British Journal of Obstetrics and Gynecology* showed that estriol had less potential to cause blood clots than synthetic estrogen over 12 months of therapy. They found "*no* significant changes in concentration of plasma coagulation factors."[23]

- *Study 2.* A Japanese study showed estriol at 2 milligrams per day improved HDLs, decreased triglycerides and total cholesterol, and therefore produced a "significant improvement in overall cardiac risk profile." This improvement occurred in women aged 70 to 84. Estriol did not improve the risk profile of the younger women in the study.[24]

- *Study 3.* A Chinese study using a synthetic long-acting form of estriol found no increase in cardiac lipids and an improvement in HDLs (good cholesterol).[25]

Discussion

None of the studies reviewed by this author showed any adverse cardiac or clotting effects in response to estriol use. Two small studies suggest possible improvement of cardiac risk factors with estriol, but these studies were on a small number of women. Of course, a large-scale study would be helpful in clarifying this matter. At worst, however, estriol would be cardiac neutral with signs of lower risk for blood clots as noted in the study from the *British Journal of Obstetrics and Gynecology*.

Given the recent results of the Women's Health Initiative (WHI), which indicate that conjugated estrogen plus synthetic progestin increase cardiac risk and breast cancer risk, and given that estriol appears to be, at worst, cardiac neutral and, at best, mildly cardiac protective, estriol appears to be the more reasonable supplement. In addition, estriol improved postmenopausal symptoms with significantly less risk for breast cancer and blood clots.

THE BOTTOM LINE

- Estriol has been shown to improve the symptoms of menopause, including hot flashes, night sweats, insomnia, depression, headache, palpitations, vaginal dryness, urinary incontinence, and loss of libido. It does so without overstimulation of breast tissue and therefore offers reduced risk of breast cancer as compared with the stronger estrogens, estrone and estradiol.
- Women with breast cancer have lower estrogen quotients (EQs) than healthy women, and this lower EQ is due to lower amounts of estriol. Women with breast cancer have estriol levels on average 30 to 60 percent lower than healthy women.
- Estriol does not strongly encourage uterine lining proliferation and in several studies did not increase uterine lining at all. For the sake of safety, let's assume that estriol does mildly increase uterine proliferation; this can be very easily offset by the addition of natural, bioidentical progesterone cream.
- Estriol reduces vaginal atrophy and urinary tract infections through direct improvement of vaginal cells and secondary improvement of vaginal pH and lactobacillus (good bacteria). Estriol also has been shown to have direct improvement in the health of urethral cells (urine tube).
- Estriol does not protect bone density as well as the strong estrogens, but when you combine it with natural progesterone and/or salmon calcitonin, you get safer control of postmenopausal symptoms plus improvement in bone mineral density (BMD).

- Estriol improves skin elastin and collagen when applied directly to the skin. More than likely, it improves skin elasticity better than no estrogen supplementation at all.
- Estriol appears to be cardiac neutral at worst and possibly mildly cardiac protective, although more studies need to be done to definitively show estriol's effect on cardiac lipids. Estriol does not appear to increase the risk of blood clots (in any of the literature reviewed by this author), as opposed to the stronger estrogens, estrone (E1) and estradiol (E2), both of which have increased risk of blood clots as known side effects.

Can I give you an ironclad guarantee that estriol at any dose will never increase the risk of breast or uterine cancer for you? The answer is no. As I've already said, every woman is a unique individual. Estriol still acts as an estrogen, and at high doses, the possibility remains that it could increase your risk of cancer by overstimulating your breast tissue. What we have done in this step is outline a program of safer ERT using estriol, which I hope will benefit millions of women whose symptoms are not controlled with other supplements or phytonutrients. As you will find throughout this book, my recommendation is to try diet and/or phytonutrient supplementation first. Then if your symptoms cannot be controlled, a trial of low-dose estriol cream may be considered. If you use estriol therapy, you should continue to have close surveillance, including breast checks, mammograms, and Pap smears (as well as uterine ultrasounds or biopsies, if indicated). For those of you on low-dose strong estrogen replacement (that is, estrone, estradiol, or conjugated estrogens), a slow taper with changes in your diet and possibly the addition of a phytonutrient supplement is in order.

Of course, only attempt to taper off your estrogen under a doctor's supervision. The doctor you use must be familiar with natural therapies, phytonutrients, and estriol. For those of you on high-dose estrogen replacement at 1.25 milligrams and higher, a switch to estriol is strongly recommended. Remember, estriol is not as strong as estrone, estradiol, or conjugated estrogens, so you may have to start at 2.5 to 5 milligrams per day of estriol cream for symptom control. In a few months, if your symptoms have been well controlled, you can try slowly titrating down under the supervision of your physician.

For the millions of you who have stopped all ERT because of the fear generated by the WHI and are now living in misery, there is a way to restore your quality of life with lower risks than your old ERT. If you stopped your ERT and are having mild symptoms, try changing your diet. And if that doesn't work, consider adding a phytonutrient supplement (see Step 6). If diet changes and natural phytonutrients do not control your symptoms, then consider the addition of low-dose estriol. Continuing your dietary changes and phytonutrients will help you stay on the lowest level of estriol possible.

WHAT IF YOU'VE ALREADY HAD BREAST CANCER?

This is a more difficult decision. If you are currently on conjugated estrogens, estrone, and/or estradiol, you should switch to estriol. In my opinion, estriol represents a far safer supplement for you than the stronger estrogens. Many of you are not on any replacement, and millions of you are miserable. The place to begin is with your diet (see Step 6). If your quality of life is still poor, even with dietary changes, consider a phytonutrient supplement, since these are the weakest forms of natural estrogen supplementation. Of course, all this should be done under the supervision of a physician who understands natural therapies. As you will see from our discussion of phytonutrients (Step 6), most studies suggest that phytonutrient supplements are associated with lower risk of breast cancer. Remember, there are no absolute guarantees. All we can say is that phytonutrient supplementation appears to be lower in risk than any estrogen supplementation.

Finally, if you need estrogen replacement to maintain a reasonable quality of life, then estriol is by far the safest choice. (There is even a fascinating study showing that not only does estriol not increase the risk of breast cancer but it *may* be a cancer therapy. This is only one small study, however, and the use of ERT in someone who has had a previous breast cancer should be a last resort.) It is always an extremely difficult question for both you and your doctor. Most doctors will say no estrogen of any type, and I would agree. Most doctors will try selective estrogen receptor modulators (SERMs), including tamoxifen and raloxifene.Unfortunately, these do not decrease menopausal symptoms.

SO WHY DOESN'T EVERY DOCTOR KNOW ABOUT ESTRIOL?

When estrogen was first discovered, it was felt that estriol was too weak to be of any consequence. Therefore, it was ignored. Around the mid-1950s, it started being used as an estrogen replacement in Europe. Slowly, studies were reported that showed estriol's usefulness and its safety. These studies were conducted mostly in Europe. The European studies were mostly ignored in the United States for two reasons: (1) Estriol did not appear to protect bone as well as other estrogen replacement therapies, and bone protection was a very "hot item" in the 1970s. (2) Most doctors in the United States get their information from pharmaceutical companies, either directly or indirectly. They receive information directly through studies conducted and funded by the pharmaceutical corporations and indirectly through studies conducted at major universities, most of which are funded by the pharmaceutical industry and/or governmental entities. The U.S. government agencies have been very closely tied to and very protective of the pharmaceutical industry. Estriol cannot be patented; therefore, no company stands to gain billions of dollars by investing the millions of dollars it costs to do extensive studies. Conjugated estrogens, estrone, and estradiol all could be patented, and pharmaceutical companies could and did do extensive studies on these ERTs and spread the word to doctors about the benefits of these strong estrogens. Doctors were told that the strong ERTs were the treatment of choice, and very few questioned whether or not this was true. Even in the last two decades, when evidence started to surface that strong ERT may increase the risk of breast cancer, doctors still wanted to believe what they were being told, and most did not question if there were safer alternative treatments available. This is a shame, since estriol had been safely used in Europe for nearly half a century. That having been said, even though this is the twenty-first century, most American doctors still are not taught about estriol!

WHAT'S THE CORRECT DOSE OF ESTRIOL?

You and your physician should consider the following:

- Begin with 0.5 milligram of estriol cream every other day. If menopausal symptoms continue, increase slowly up to between 2 and 5 milligrams every other day, depending on response.

  If symptoms aren't controlled on an every-other-day treatment regimen, increase to daily doses. Every 3 to 6 months, try to slightly reduce your dose to see if it is tolerated. If symptoms return, you can return to your previous dose.
- Topical estriol is absorbed twenty times more effectively than the oral (pill) form. Therefore, always use the topical (cream) form.
- If vaginal atrophy and urinary problems are your major complaints, estriol cream can be compounded for vaginal use.
- If you are unable to control your symptoms at 5 milligrams of estriol daily, combination products are available that consist of 80 percent estriol and 20 percent estradiol. (Example: If 1.25 milligrams is prescribed per day, 1 milligram is estriol and 0.25 milligram is estradiol. This combination is stronger than estriol and should help to control symptoms not controlled by pure estriol. Remember, the stronger the estrogen, the higher the risks of side effects and/or breast cancer. It is thought, however, that if the majority of this cream is estriol, the estriol will

bind to the estrogen receptors in your breasts and help protect them against the stronger estradiol.
- Don't use oral estrogen replacement if possible.
- Don't use estriol if you are pregnant or breast-feeding.
- Don't use estriol if you have had previous breast or ovarian cancer.
- Use only professionally formulated topical or vaginal creams.
- Reduce or discontinue estriol if you develop severe breast tenderness, increased breast fibrocysts, or excessive vaginal bleeding.
- Balance estriol with bioidentical progesterone cream. The progesterone can be placed in the same cream with the estriol. (See Step 8.)
- Always use the lowest dose that relieves symptoms, and try small reductions in your dose every 6 months.
- Work with a physician who understands estriol therapy. Most physicians will be ignorant of what you are trying to tell them, and most physicians resist taking suggestions from patients.

     Finding the right physician may take a little work, but it is well worth the effort!
- Every woman is unique. Therefore, your dose will be different from anyone else's. Your response to the medication and/or side effects will be on an individual basis. The time for one-size-fits-all treatments, I hope, is coming to an end. It is vital that you work with a physician or health care practitioner who understands these principles.
- Read the rest of this book!

In the next step, we'll talk about the estrogen metabolite index (EMI). As you will see, it's not just the type of estrogen you take and/or make, but how you detoxify it that determines your breast cancer risk. We'll review the two predominant estrogen metabolites and how one metabolite, the 2 OH, can protect your breasts, while the other metabolite, 16 OH, significantly *increases* your risk of breast cancer.

Find Out Your Estrogen Metabolite Index

All estrogen, whether produced naturally or given as a prescription, gets broken down in your liver via an enzyme system named the P450 pathway. This P450 system detoxifies many substances, including hormones, medicines, and toxins. The detoxification of your stronger estrogens occurs along two major pathways within this P450 system (see Figure 4.1).

THE ESTROGEN PATHWAYS

Estrone (E1) and estradiol (E2) are converted to three distinct types of metabolites. (As mentioned earlier, a metabolite is a by-product of any type of metabolism.) These metabolites are 2-hydroxyestrone (2 OH), 4-hydroxyestrone (4 OH), and 16-hydroxyestrone (16 OH). No woman converts down one pathway alone. You convert a portion of your estrogen down each pathway. The important question is, How much estrogen do you convert down the 2 OH pathway (which *lowers* your breast cancer risk) versus the 16 OH pathway (which *increases* your risk)? We will discuss these metabolites in great detail.

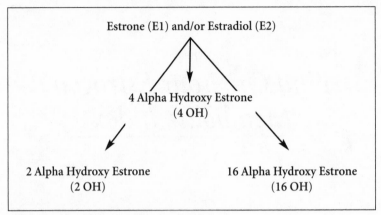

Figure 4.1 Estrogen Detoxification Pathways

Why do you have to detoxify estrogen in the first place? If estrogen was not detoxified (metabolized), it would quickly build up in your system and overstimulate all the tissues that are sensitive to it. These include your breasts, ovaries, uterus, and brain. This overstimulation would rapidly lead to significant symptoms, including heavy bleeding, fibrocystic breast disease, and breast cancer. It is vital for the body to maintain a balance of estrogen—not too much, not too little. This is true for nearly everything in nature and certainly for all hormones.

The majority of your estrogen follows two major pathways. The 16 OH pathway produces the 16 OH metabolite, which retains strong estrogen activity. In fact, many researchers feel that 16 OH is actually more potent and more dangerous than estrogen itself! Studies have shown that overproduction of 16 OH *significantly increases* your risk of breast cancer.

Why does the 16 OH metabolite significantly increase cancer risk? The 16 OH metabolite acts as a strong estrogen even though it is a metabolite. The stronger the stimulation of your breast tissue by strong metabolites, the greater the risk of overstimulation, which could lead to cancers.

As we reviewed in Step 2, the job of estrogen is to stimulate breast tissue growth. Without estrogen stimulation, your breasts would not have developed in the first place, and without estrogen, breast health could not be maintained. However, overstimulation causes rapid overproduction of breast cells. If you combine the overstimulation of breast cells with a lack of control due to DNA (genetic) damage, the breast cells begin to reproduce in an out-of-control manner, leading to breast cancer. There is also some evidence that the 16 OH metabolite may stay bound to the estrogen receptors in your breasts for a long time. This would cause chronic stimulation, which, as stated above, when combined with damage to your breast cell genes could be the start of cancer.

The 2 OH pathway, however, has been associated with a *lower* risk of breast cancer. Low levels of the 2 OH metabolite have been associated with lower levels of all female cancer, including breast cancer.[1]

The 2 OH metabolite has low estrogenic activity. This means that when 2 OH binds to the estrogen receptors in your breasts, it causes slower, more orderly cell reproduction. This makes it less likely that breast cell reproduction will run wild. In addition, if the 2 OH metabolite is bound to an estrogen receptor, 16 OH cannot bind to the same receptor. Only one estrogen metabolite or estrogen molecule can bind to an estrogen receptor at one time. 2 OH, therefore, helps maintain the necessary stimulation for breast health while protecting against the overstimulation that would occur if the 16 OH metabolite were attached to the estrogen receptor.[2]

WHAT DO THE STUDIES TELL US?

Medical studies have shown that the lower your 2 OH/16 OH ratio, especially if it is below 2, the *higher* your risk of breast cancer. What is the optimal 2 OH/16 OH ratio? No one knows the answer to this question. But research has shown that the closer your 2 OH/16 OH ratio is to 2, the *less* your risk of breast cancer. The closer your ratio is to 1, the *greater* your risk. So the most desirable outcome of this ratio is: 2 OH ÷ 16 OH = 2 or above. This answer is known as your estrogen metabolite index (EMI). Therefore, your EMI should be 2 or above.

- *Study 1.* Postmenopausal women who went on to develop breast cancer had an EMI 15 percent lower than women without breast cancer.[3] The women with the highest third 2 OH/16 OH ratio (EMI) had a 30 percent lower risk of developing breast cancer than those in the lower two-thirds. Essentially, this study showed that if you maintain your 2 OH/16 OH ratio in the highest third of all women, you may reduce your risk of breast cancer by 30 percent. This study also showed that women with EMI scores of 2 had less breast cancer than women with the lower score of 1.5! It is apparent that even small improvements in the EMI makes a huge difference. In fact, a separate 1998 study indicated that EMI was *the most significant predictive factor of breast cancer in postmenopausal women.*[4]
- *Study 2.* In postmenopausal women with breast cancer, the 2 OH/16 OH ratio (EMI) was 1.4 versus 1.7 for women of the same age who did not have breast cancer.

This study confirms that a ratio closer to 2 appears to be significantly safer than a ratio closer to 1.[5]

Discussion

These studies show that if you can keep your 2 OH/16 OH ratio (EMI) at 2 or above, you may have a 30 percent lower risk of breast cancer than if you allow your 2 OH/16 OH ratio (EMI) to drop to 1.5 or below. What happens if your ratio is lower than 1? These studies did not specifically discuss the risk to a woman who had a ratio below 1. Most researchers believe that the lower your EMI, the higher your risk of breast cancer. In clinical practice, I have seen women with ratios as low as 0.2! These women had a 2 OH/16 OH ratio (EMI) one-tenth the optimal level. Trust me; this is not where you want to be.

WHY WOULD YOUR 2 OH/16 OH RATIO (EMI) BE LOW?

There are two primary reasons for having a low EMI: genetics and environment.

Genetics

A small percentage of women have genetic problems with the conversion of estrogen to the 2 OH metabolite. Studies have shown that certain groups of women have a significantly reduced ability to convert estrogen to the 2 OH even when they are given natural supplements that usually improve this conversion.[6] Why these groups have this genetic abnormality and what can be done about it is not known at this time. Thankfully only a small segment of women have a genetic problem with this conversion; for most women it is a problem with environmental factors (which can be improved).

Environment

There are many environmental factors that hinder the conversion of estrogen to the 2 OH metabolite. If you have reduced amounts of the nutrients necessary to make your P450 pathway run optimally, you will detoxify estrogen more poorly or convert it to the wrong type of metabolite (that is, to the 16 OH metabolite). We will discuss the nutrients necessary for proper liver detoxification at length in later steps. The important point here is that there is a tremendous amount that you can do to improve detoxification of estrogen and shift your detoxification toward the 2 OH pathway. This will cause your 2 OH/16 OH ratio (EMI) to increase, with your goal being 2 or slightly above. Remember, your estrogen metabolite index (2 OH/16 OH ratio) is one of the most important predictive factor for breast cancer in postmenopausal women. This makes improving your EMI *vital* if you have a ratio below 2.

Are There Medications That Affect the 2 OH/16 OH Ratio (EMI)?
Certain medications decrease 2 OH and increase 16 OH. One example is cimetidine.[7] If you have recurrent indigestion and require cimetidine or similar medications frequently, you should

work on food allergy avoidance, so that you can work toward reducing your reflux and/or heartburn and therefore reduce your need for cimetidine and similar medications. This will help to improve your 2 OH/16 OH ratio. (For a complete discussion of chronic reflux, bowel dysbiosis, and food allergies, see *America Exhausted, Breakthrough Treatments of Fatigue and Fibromyalgia*, Vitality Press, 1998.)

HOW DO YOU KNOW WHAT YOUR 2 OH/16 OH RATIO (EMI) IS?

This is the amazing part of our story. Finding out your EMI is easy and relatively inexpensive. This is accomplished via a simple urine test, where we measure the amount of 2 OH and the amount of 16 OH in your urine.

In the clinic, I recommend to most women that they obtain a 24-hour urine study (levels done on a 24-hour collection are more accurate than those done on a single sample), which will not only give your EMI but will also tell you the levels of your three different estrogens.

This will allow you to determine your estrogen quotient (EQ), which can be important for reducing your breast cancer risk. (If you can't get the 24-hour test, then do the one-time EMI.) If your EMI isn't 2 or above, you can make the appropriate changes in your diet and/or add nutritional supplements to increase your ratio. If you ask your doctor for a test of your 2 OH/16 OH ratio, you might get a very puzzled or condescending look; many doctors are simply not aware of this extremely helpful test.

HOW OFTEN SHOULD YOU HAVE YOUR
2 OH/16 OH RATIO (EMI) CHECKED?

Always have your ratio checked before starting supplemental estrogen. In my opinion, every woman should know what her EMI is. If it is below 2 on your first check, you should recheck it about every 6 months, until it rises to 2 or above. Once you are on a stable program aimed at increasing your EMI and your ratio has improved to 2 or above, then you can check it yearly or every other year.

IMPROVING YOUR 2 OH/16 OH RATIO (EMI)

There are several important steps you can take to improve your EMI if it is below 2.

- *Improve your diet.* Eating more of the nutrients that help you to convert your estrogen to the "good" 2 OH metabolite is an easy first step to take. These nutrients include the cruciferous vegetables that we will discuss at length in the next step.
- *Improve liver detoxification.* Many of you are low in the antioxidants necessary to promote optimal detoxification of estrogen. We will discuss those nutrients in detail in several of the later steps.
- *Increase your intake of I3C or DIM.* These are nutrients that actually shift your detoxification of estrogen in favor of the 2 OH metabolite. This increases your 2 OH/16 OH ratio (EMI), which is what we have been discussing

throughout this step. For a complete discussion of I3C
and DIM, see Step 5.
- *Increase your intake of antioxidants.* Many antioxidants
protect your breast cells from damage, and we will discuss them at length in later steps.

THE BOTTOM LINE

There is a tremendous amount you can do to improve your
2 OH/16 OH ratio (EMI). These steps are relatively easy and fairly
inexpensive. We will review them in detail throughout the remainder of this book. The important point to take away from this step
is that you must know what your 2 OH/16 OH ratio is. If it is above
2, terrific! If it is below 2, then you need to take steps to improve
that ratio to 2 or above. This may reduce your risk of breast cancer
by 30 percent or more. The lower your EMI, the greater your risk
of breast cancer, the more carefully your ratio should be monitored,
and the more aggressively you should work to improve your ratio.
This is something that premenopausal women can do to reduce
their risk just as easily and effectively as postmenopausal women.
For women of any age, knowing your EMI is vital. Working to make
sure it is 2 or above is one of the simple things you can do to significantly reduce your breast cancer risk.

Before we move on to discussing the nutrients that are important for improving your EMI, let's review the third metabolite
in Figure 4.1 on page 44. That metabolite is 4 OH (4-hydroxye-
strone). The body converts estrogen predominantly to either the
2 OH or the 16 OH metabolite, with only a small amount being
converted to 4 OH. Despite its relatively small amount, 4 OH is

known to increase breast cancer risk. 4 OH appears to be a free radical generator and may be extremely destructive if you are low in substances that "quench" free radicals. Examples of free radical "quenchers" are folic acid and the tri-amino acid glutathione. As you already know, the more damage to your DNA, the greater the chances of mutations, which can lead to breast cancer. 4 OH has also been shown to cause breast cancer in human tissue culture.[8] We will discuss folic acid more a little later in Step 14. It is one of those easy, cheap supplements you can use to significantly reduce your breast cancer risk. Making sure your levels of folic acid stay high may be one way to reduce the free radical damage that 4 OH produces. Because there are no known adverse side effects to folic acid at even large doses and it is relatively inexpensive, to me this seems like a "no brainer." Glutathione is a very important antioxidant and we will discuss how to improve your glutathione levels in Step 17.

We will now review in detail the nutrients that are available to reduce "bad"16 OH metabolite formation and increase the "good" 2 OH metabolite. Let's move on to the next step and discuss I3C and DIM and see how those breakthrough nutrients may help reduce your risk of breast cancer by 90 percent or more.

Increase Your Intake of I3C and DIM: Nature's Secret Weapons

What are I3C and DIM? I3C (indole-3-carbinol) is a phytonutrient found in cruciferous vegetables. (For a list of cruciferous vegetables, see Table 5.1.) For years it has been observed that countries that consume more cruciferous vegetables have a lower breast cancer rate than countries that consume less. Until recently, no one has really known why. The reason appears to be that these vegetables contain the phytonutrient I3C. When you eat cruciferous vegetables containing I3C, your stomach acid converts the I3C to many different compounds. One of those is DIM (diindolylmethane).

HOW I3C AND DIM CAN REDUCE YOUR RISK OF BREAST CANCER

I3C and DIM can reduce your risk of breast cancer in three ways: by improving the way you metabolize estrogen, by improving the function of your tumor suppressor genes, and by blocking cancer-causing chemicals from attaching to the estrogen receptors in your breasts.

Table 5.1 Cruciferous Vegetables

Bok choy	Collards
Broccoli	Kale
Brussels sprouts	Rutabagas
Cabbage	Turnips
Cauliflower	Watercress

Effect on Estrogen Metabolism

I3C and DIM improve the way you metabolize estrogen. In the last step, we discussed how estrogen is mainly converted to two metabolites, 2 OH and 16 OH. We discovered that if you convert estrogen predominately to the 16 OH metabolite, your risk of breast cancer *increases*. We also discovered that if you convert more of your estrogen to the 2 OH metabolite, your risk of developing breast cancer *decreases*. You learned how important your 2 OH/16 OH ratio (estrogen metabolite index, or EMI) is to cancer prevention. I3C and DIM are two natural substances that improve your 2 OH/16 OH ratio. I3C and DIM improve the conversion of estrogen to the 2 OH metabolite. It does this by increasing the process that converts the strong estrogens (estradiol and estrone) to 2 OH. When you eat vegetables that contain I3C, that I3C is converted in your stomach to DIM, and the DIM shifts your conversion toward the "good" 2 OH metabolite and away from the "bad" 16 OH metabolite. This, by definition, improves your 2 OH/16 OH ratio. Because I3C/DIM helps to convert your estrogen toward the "good" 2 OH metabolite, there is less estrogen available to be converted to the "bad" 16 OH metabolite. Studies have shown that I3C works quickly to increase the conversion of estrogen to the 2 OH, and no major side effects were noted.[1]

A study of 60 women showed the 2 OH/16 OH ratio increased for the women on I3C (400 milligrams a day) and stayed up for as long as they took the I3C without apparent harmful side effects. In another study published in the *Journal of the National Cancer Institute*, 10 women given 400 milligrams of I3C for 2 months had an increased amount of 2 OH, and the levels of strong estrogen and 16 OH went down.[2] (See Figure 5.1.)

This study showed that I3C reduced estradiol, estrone, and the 16 OH metabolite. It should be noted that not only will the reduction in 16 OH improve your EMI, but the reduction of estradiol and estrone will also improve your estrogen quotient (EQ). Both of these changes powerfully reduce your risk of breast cancer.

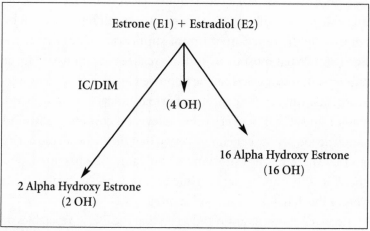

Figure 5.1 Improvement of the 2 OH Pathway by I3C/DIM

Effect on Tumor Suppressor Genes

I3C and DIM improve the function of tumor suppressor genes. I3C and DIM appear to work on both estrogen receptor positive (ER positive) breast cancer cells and estrogen receptor negative (ER negative) breast cancer cells. ER positive breast cancer cells require estrogen to allow them to grow. Having ER positive breast cancer cells is actually a good thing, because that means the cancer is more likely to respond to antiestrogen therapies. (ER negative breast cancers, on the other hand, do not require the presence of estrogen to grow and therefore respond much more poorly to estrogen receptor modulating agents, such as tamoxifen and raloxifene.) I3C actually works on ER negative breast cancer cells by being able to turn up your cancer suppressor genes.[3]

Remember from Step 1 that cancer suppressor genes slow breast cell reproduction and are responsible for keeping cell reproduction under control. What these studies tell us is that I3C was actually able to slow ER negative breast cancer cell reproduction by improving the function of tumor suppressor genes that work against it. What most doctors don't realize is that breast cancer tumor suppressor genes can be improved by both foods and supplements. You can bet that if a pharmaceutical company held a patent on I3C/DIM, every other television commercial would "inform you" of the benefits of taking that medicine. Because I3C and DIM are natural substances and cannot be patented, and therefore little money can be made, no one is bothering to inform you of the benefits of these substances.

Research shows us again and again that the I3C in vegetables or the I3C/DIM by supplement may improve how your tumor suppressor genes function and may therefore significantly reduce your risk of breast cancer. If this wasn't enough of a reason to eat cruciferous vegetables, we also know that I3C can decrease the activity of invasive breast cancer cells.[4] Invasive breast cancer is the most dangerous type of breast cancer and the type that is most likely to kill you. So the studies have shown that I3C can turn up tumor suppressor genes *and* reduce the chance that, if you develop a breast tumor, it will invade the surrounding normal tissue.

Effect on Cancer-Causing Chemicals

I3C and DIM may block cancer-causing chemicals from attaching to the estrogen receptors in your breasts. I3C and DIM bind to the aryl hydrocarbon receptor in your breast cells. The aryl hydrocarbon receptor, also known as the "Ah" receptor, is the receptor for stimulating cell growth—which also means it can stimulate cancer cells. When chemicals such as dioxin, which are toxic by-products of industrial processes, attach themsselves to the "Ah" receptor, they cause breast cells to reproduce wildly, eventually resulting in a tumor.[5] (We will discuss dioxin at length in Step 13. There you will see that dioxin is nearly everywhere, including our food. So most of you have dioxin in you now and consume small amounts of dioxin daily.)

If I3C is attached to the "Ah" receptor, dioxins cannot bind. If dioxin cannot bind, it cannot overstimulate breast cells, and breast cell reproduction stays at a normal level. Clearly, having I3C attached to the "Ah" receptor is a very good thing indeed! Not only do dioxins appear to activate cancer growth genes, but they also *suppress* tumor suppressor genes. Studies show that I3C appears to dramatically lower the effects of dioxin on breast cells.[6] Unfortunately, I3C does not stay bound to the "Ah" receptor for long periods of time. Therefore, you need to take small amounts of I3C/DIM on a regular basis to maintain its blocking effect on dioxin and other chemicals. That's why eating foods that contain I3C daily or several times a week is important. You get small amounts of I3C on a regular basis. If you take a supplement, small amounts daily are better than larger amounts less frequently.

DIINDOLYLMETHANE: A METABOLITE OF I3C

We have been using I3C and DIM (diindolylmethane) interchangeably throughout this step. Let's review briefly what DIM is and the differences between I3C and DIM. DIM is one of the active metabolites of I3C. I3C does not appear to have direct effects in the body until it is transformed into a metabolite. When you eat vegetables that contain I3C, stomach acid is needed to convert the I3C to its metabolites. The amount of stomach acid determines what metabolites you make. If your stomach acid is low, you have more difficulty utilizing I3C; your conversion of I3C to DIM is less efficient, and you don't reap as many benefits from the I3C. Despite what the commercials are constantly telling you, millions of you have low stomach acid, especially if you are over the age of 40. One of the ironies of life is that low stomach acid can actually create many of the same symptoms that high stomach acid creates: poor digestion, indigestion, bloating, and gas. Lack of proper stomach acid causes poor absorption of many nutrients, including I3C. In addition, millions of you are on acid-suppressive medications for chronic acid reflux disease. These medications reduce the absorption of I3C by lowering stomach acid. Unfortunately, physicians prescribe these acid-suppressive medications routinely instead of looking for the real cause of the chronic reflux, which in many cases is a chronic food allergy, a bacterial infection such as *H. pylori*, a yeast infection such as candida, and/or lack of digestive enzymes. If you are on an acid-suppressive medication, you will have difficulty converting I3C to DIM; therefore, a DIM supplement may be required.

Even under conditions of normal stomach pH, only a small percentage of I3C is converted to DIM.[7] As we briefly reviewed, I3C is converted not only to DIM but also to many other phytochemicals. The effects of these phytochemical metabolites are not well known at this time, and there is considerable controversy surrounding them. There is the concern that in high doses, side effects of I3C could occur. For example, one of the metabolites from I3C may increase the conversion of estrogen to the 4 OH metabolite. And as we saw in the last step, 4 OH has been associated with an increased risk of breast cancer and/or uterine tumors. With this in mind, increasing levels of all metabolites of I3C may not be such a great idea.

Studies have shown that DIM supplements improve the production of the "good" 2 OH metabolite by increasing the activity of the enzymes that convert estrogen to 2 OH.[8] Research has shown that DIM supplements block the "Ah" receptor as effectively as natural DIM after it has been metabolized from I3C. DIM improves your EMI (2 OH/16 OH) at a lower dose than I3C and with fewer possible side effects. Most research points to DIM as being the most important breakdown product of I3C. It is up to ten times more active than I3C, so smaller amounts need to be taken if a supplement is used.[9] So for the millions of people with low stomach acid either through age-related decline or reduction via acid-suppressive medication, a DIM supplement might be the way to go, since (unlike I3C) it does not require stomach acid for absorption.

I3C VERSUS DIM: THE CONTROVERSY

Recently, a controversy has developed as to which is the superior supplement: I3C or DIM. The group that supports I3C believes that several of the other breakdown products of I3C besides DIM may be important for breast cancer prevention. They point out that when you take a DIM supplement, you only get DIM and that if other breakdown products are important, you would miss out on those benefits.

The other group, including the company that owns the patent on absorbable DIM, counters with studies that show that certain metabolites of I3C, such as indolocarbazole (ICZ) and ascorbigen (ASB), may increase the production of the 4 OH metabolite, which increases the risk of breast cancer.[9,10] Furthermore, they feel that since DIM appears to be responsible for many, if not all, of the positive effects of I3C on estrogen detoxification and since DIM appears safer, it should be the supplement of choice.

This becomes problematic only if you decide to use supplemental I3C or DIM to improve your 2 OH/16 OH ratio. It should be noted that the cruciferous vegetables contain I3C, which is then converted in your stomach to DIM, along with multiple other metabolites, and since eating cruciferous vegetables is the most natural treatment, this is where you should start. I recognize, however, that many of you will not eat cruciferous vegetables and will want the ease or convenience of taking a supplement. In addition, some of you may have a very low EMI and may not be able to eat enough of the cruciferous vegetables to improve your ratio to our target, which is 2 or above. For you, supplementation with I3C or DIM would be reasonable. DIM has the following positive points:

- It improves 2 OH and therefore raises your EMI (2 Oh/16 OH ratio).
- Small doses are required to obtain an effect, so the possibility of side effects is reduced.
- DIM has the ability to block the "Ah" receptor in your breasts and therefore protect your breasts from the dangerous/toxic effects of chemicals like dioxin.
- It is unclear from studies if DIM improves BRCA1 tumor suppressor function, but since it is the major active metabolite of I3C, it would stand to reason that it does. Further studies on this issue need to be conducted.
- H. Leon Bradlow, Ph.D., of the Strang Cancer Research Center in New York, one of the pioneer researchers on the effects of I3C on estrogen metabolism, has come out publicly in favor of DIM as opposed to I3C as a supplement. Although much of Dr. Bradlow's original research focused on I3C, he feels, after reviewing new research, that DIM is the safer supplement.[11]

THE BOTTOM LINE

- Know your EMI (2 OH/16 OH ratio).
- If your EMI is below 2, add as many of the cruciferous vegetables to your diet as possible (moderate amounts daily).
- If your ratio does not improve to 2 or you are unable or unwilling to eat cruciferous vegetables, then consider adding low doses of bioavailable DIM, beginning at 75 milligrams once daily. Recheck your EMI in 6 months. If you decide to use I3C, then keep the dose low or consider a combination I3C/DIM supplement that contains low doses of each.)
- If upon recheck, your EMI is still below 2, consider increasing your DIM to 150 milligrams per day and recheck your ratio in 6 months.
- Once your EMI is 2 or above, you should recheck it yearly. Women with extremely low levels of EMI may not be able to get their ratio up to 2; however, these women still may improve their EMI nearly tenfold, which will significantly lower their breast cancer risk. Remember, improving your EMI takes time; therefore it makes sense to check the EMI every 6 to 12 months.

General Guidelines

- *Never* use DIM or I3C if you are pregnant or breast-feeding. Although there are no studies showing that they are toxic, there also are no human studies on the safety

of DIM/I3C during pregnancy or breast-feeding. Therefore, avoid it.
- Exercise caution using DIM/I3C and birth control pills
(oral contraceptives). No formal studies of DIM/I3C and
birth control pills have been completed. If you wish to use
DIM/I3C, then use alternative birth control methods.
- Always take DIM/I3C with food.

Possible Side Effects of DIM Supplements

- *Gas.* If you get your I3C through cruciferous vegetables,
there is very little risk of side effects, except perhaps
excessive gas.
- *Headaches.* Occasional headaches have been noted with
DIM. If this happens, reduce your dose until the
headaches subside; then increase the dose more slowly.
- *Nausea.* If this occurs, it is usually relieved by taking
DIM with food.
- *Diarrhea.* This is rare, but if it happens, reduce your dose.
- *Urine color.* Urine color may change to amber.
This is harmless but should lessen if you increase your
fluid intake.

Use Phytoestrogens to Protect Yourself from Breast Cancer

What are phytoestrogens, and how do they help protect you from breast cancer? The word *phytoestrogen* is actually a misnomer (the prefix *phyto* means "plants"), since plants do not make estrogen; only animals produce true estrogen. Phytoestrogens are nutrients in certain plants whose chemical structure allows them to bind with your estrogen receptors. These substances, in many cases, have chemical structures that are similar to estradiol. These phytoestrogens occur in nature as two major classes: isoflavones and lignans. Isoflavones are found predominantly in the legume family, and this includes soy. Lignans are found in whole grains, legumes, vegetables, and seeds—especially flaxseed.

WHAT DO THE STUDIES TELL US?

The medical literature shows that women who have higher levels of phytoestrogens in their urine have a significantly reduced risk of breast cancer. One study published in the *British Medical Journal* showed that there was a *fourfold* risk reduction for women with the highest 25 percent levels of phytoestrogen versus the women with the lowest 25 percent levels of phytoestrogen. This study also showed that the women who had the highest levels of the phytoestrogen enterolactone were at one-third the risk of breast cancer as the women who had the lowest levels. *One-third the risk!* According to the study, these results were true for both premenopausal and postmenopausal women.[1] These statistics are quite amazing.

Two other studies showed that phytoestrogen levels were lower in women with breast cancer than in the control groups, which were made up of women approximately the same age but without breast cancer.[2]

A fascinating study appeared in 2002 in the journal *Carcinogenesis*. This study found that Asian-American women who reported eating soy every week when they were children and now as adults had a *47 percent* reduction in breast cancer risk compared with those who ate low levels of soy. (Soy has very high levels of the phytoestrogens called isoflavones.) For the women who ate high levels of soy as adolescents but now eat low levels as an adult, the risk was still *23 percent* lower. The highest level of risk reduction was found in women who ate the most soy.[3] There is clearly a link between isoflavones and a decreased risk of breast cancer.

Even more interesting, a study published in the *Journal of Cancer, Epidemiology, Biomarkers and Prevention* showed that postmenopausal Asian women who ate soy-based foods regularly as part of their diet had lower levels of estrone compared with women who did not eat soy.[4] This is an important point, for as we have discussed, estrone is a strong estrogen that lowers your estrogen quotient and may increase your risk of breast cancer.

Are you starting to get the impression that it would be to your benefit to be in the group of women highest in soy consumption? One study shows you can reduce your risk by four times, another shows a 47 percent reduction in risk, and two others show phytoestrogen levels lowest in women with breast cancer.

Why Do Women Who Consume High Levels of Phytoestrogens Have Lower Breast Cancer Risks?

We have known for decades that Asian women have a significantly lower breast cancer incidence, as compared with women who eat a Western diet. We now, through medical studies, appear to know some of the reasons why. We have evidence from the real world and evidence from the research world why increasing your levels of phytoestrogens is logical and beneficial.

Phytoestrogens Bind Estrogen Receptors

When phytonutrients are bound to the estrogen receptors, they exert a weak estrogen-like activity and reduce the amount of strong estrogens that can attach. This blocks estradiol, estrone, and 16 OH metabolites from binding and therefore overstimulating your breast tissue. We have already discussed that estradiol, estrone, and 16 OH are strong stimulators of cell reproduction. You know that overstimulation by these strong estrogens can cause cellular reproduction to go out of control, which, if there is DNA damage, can eventually result in a tumor. If you keep many of the estrogen receptors occupied by a weak estrogenic substance, you may significantly reduce the possibility of overstimulation from the strong estrogens and estrogen metabolites. This reduces your cancer risk. For years researchers have wondered why Japanese women have a significantly lower risk of breast cancer compared with American women.

Yet, when Asian women adopt a Western diet—which often is low in phytoestrogens—their breast cancer elevates to the Western level within two generations.[5] Breast cancer rates have historically been four to seven times higher in the United States than in China or Japan.

Sadly, this will probably change as we send the children of China and Japan burgers, fries, and other fast food. As that generation drifts away from the traditional diet, we can expect their level of breast cancer to start going up exponentially.

Studies have shown that the lower frequency of breast cancer in Asian women is not genetic: when these women moved to the United States and changed their diet, they also raised their risk of breast cancer. Almost certainly the increase in risk is secondary to diet and other environmental factors.

Many studies have shown that Asian women consume large amounts of the foods that contain phytoestrogens, particularly soy products like tofu, soy sprouts, tempeh, bean paste, and miso. Asian women have levels of phytoestrogens hundreds of times higher than levels seen inWestern women.[6] For example, many Asian women consume 20 to 80 milligrams a day of the phytoestrogen genistein—common in soy, tofu, and tempeh. The estimated amount a woman in the United States consumes of this phytoestrogen is approximately 1 to 3 milligrams daily.[7]

Phytoestrogens May Improve Your EMI

Postmenopausal women who had their diet supplemented with soy powder had increased levels of the 2 OH metabolite (the "good" metabolite) and decreased levels of 16 OH, 4 OH, and estradiol. The study suggested that "soy isoflavones may exert a cancer preventative effect by altering metabolism away from the genotoxic metabolites and toward weaker metabolites."[8]

Soy Phytoestrogens May Lower
Blood Levels of More Dangerous Estrogens

Earlier we reviewed a study published in the journal *Cancer Epidemiology, Biomarkers and Prevention* showing that eating soy foods on a regular basis lowers the blood levels of the stronger estrogen estrone. High levels of estrone have been associated with an increased risk of breast cancer.

ADDING PHYTOESTROGENS
TO YOUR DIET

The majority of women I have seen in the clinic have no problem understanding and accepting the fact that they should increase their phytonutrient intake. The problems arise when they try to do this on a day-to-day basis in the real world. In Asian countries, it is much easier, since many of their foods are soy based. Soy has become part of their culture. In the Western diet, it is quite the opposite. So let's review some easy ways to increase the phyto-estrogens in your diet.

Soy

As we've seen from the studies mentioned, the first step that you can take is to increase the soy foods in your diet. The easiest way to get soy protein is to mix soy powder with soy milk once daily in the blender. I have recommended this to women for years, since it is a cheap and easy way to get a large amount of soy isoflavones in your diet with very little fuss. Most women will mix this up in the morning and sip it with breakfast or on their way to work. They find it is very easy and convenient. In the clinic, I have not observed any side effects in the women using soy protein powder. Many women have difficulty knowing how to prepare foods made from fermented soy.

If you can eat enough fermented soy (tofu, tempeh), that appears to be the safest and the best way to get your soy. However, most Americans will not eat fermented soy foods several times a week and should therefore consider soy protein or a soy supplement (like genistein).

Recently, however, some scientists have begun to question the value of unfermented soy products. They note that the soy intake of Asian women consists overwhelmingly of foods that are fermented, such as miso, tempeh, and tofu. One long-time researcher and doctor looked back into ancient Chinese writings and found that soybeans weren't added to the Chinese diet until a process of fermentation was discovered.

Once this fermentation process was discovered, soy became a staple of the Chinese diet.[9] The question is, Why didn't the ancient Chinese eat unfermented soy foods? The answer may be that along with phytonutrients, soy also contains substances that may interfere with health.

Soy and Thyroid Function

It has been reported that unfermented soy contains substances that interfere with thyroid function. Many American women are low in thyroid function and do not know it. Many have a mild or not so mild thyroid inflammation named *thyroiditis*. Once again, fermentation appears to break down the substances that may interfere with thyroid function, allowing soy to be consumed without harmful effects on the thyroid. No large-scale studies have been conducted to find out if eating unfermented soy in large amounts is harmful, though studies have shown that animals fed unfermented soy are at an increased risk of goiter. It is also interesting that societies that have integrated soy so finely in their diet do not eat large quantities of unfermented soy.

My philosophy is that when the studies are in question or unclear, we should proceed with what has worked. We know that Asian women have a significantly lower risk of breast cancer than Western women. We also know that Asian women eat large amounts of fermented soy products and therefore consume vastly more isoflavones than women on a Western diet. Furthermore, studies have shown that these isoflavones may improve your estrogen metabolic index (EMI), improve your esrogen quotient (EQ), and bind the estrogen receptors in your breasts, not allowing the stronger estrogens to attach.

Until the question about fermented versus unfermented soy is answered, I recommend adding fermented soy products to your diet, such as tofu, miso, and tempeh. Your goal should be to add roughly 20 milligrams of genistein (from soy) per day to your overall diet. For a list of foods that contain genistein, see Table 6.1. There

Table 6.1 Foods Containing Genistein

Foods	*Genistein**
Tofu, 100 grams	15 milligrams
Tempeh, 50 grams	17 milligrams
Bean curd, 100 grams	25 milligrams
Bean paste, 100 grams	25 milligrams
Roasted soybeans, 20 grams	18 milligrams

*Approximate levels

Source: www. isoflavones.info

are many books where you can find delicious, easy recipes that will help you incorporate more soy foods into your (and your daughter's) diet. Remember the study that showed that women who started phytoestrogen foods at a young age had a significantly reduced level of breast cancer compared with women who just ate soy foods as adults. I understand that this may take some work. Probably the first food a young woman would accept and eat would be tofu, used in appropriate recipes.

Flaxseed

Flax is a major source of the phytoestrogen lignan. The usual level of lignans for a woman on a Western diet is very low. Yet when women are given just 10 grams of flaxseed powder per day, their lignan levels increased by nearly tenfold.[10] Studies of lignans in postmenopausal women showed that lignan levels were *significantly lower* in the women with breast cancer compared with normal women.[11] Clearly, there is a benefit to increasing your lignan intake!

The mechanisms for how flaxseed can reduce your risk of breast cancer are similar to those for soy. The phytoestrogens in flax (entero-lactone and enterodiol) bind to estrogen receptors in your breasts and exert very weak estrogenic activity. This estrogenic activity is one reason why postmenopausal women have found soy and flax help-ful in controlling menopausal symptoms. We will discuss this in detail a little later. As we saw with soy, if a weak phytoestrogenic substance is bound to the estrogen receptors, the stronger estrogens and estro-gen metabolites cannot bind. This lowers breast cell stimulation and keeps breast tissue reproduction at more normal levels. It is unclear at this time if flax phytoestrogens also improve your EMI. Because EMI improves with an increase in soy intake, one would suspect that they would, but no studies could be found to support this.

Flaxseed can be bought at any health food store and ground into a powder using an electric coffee grinder or food processor. This powder can be added to just about anything—soups, salads, breads, muffins, meat loaf—or eaten by itself as a warm cereal in winter. This is an extremely cheap, easy, and good-tasting way to get your phytoestrogens. I suggest to my patients that they eat one muffin a day that contains 10 grams of flax powder (homemade).

PHYTOESTROGENS AND OSTEOPOROSIS

Phytoestrogen nutrients may also play a part in preventing osteo-porosis. A study published in the *American Journal of Clinical Nutrition* showed that high levels of soy isoflavones protected against spinal bone loss.[12] Significant increases in bone mineral density occurred in the group that was given isolated soy protein every day. In addition, this study also showed that isoflavones from soy decreased the risk factors that cause heart disease.

For decades, researchers and doctors have struggled to explain a paradox (or what appeared to be a paradox). Asian women seemed to be perfect candidates for osteoporosis. They are fair-skinned, usually small-boned, and live in a northern climate. Yet the risk of osteoporosis in countries like Japan is *significantly lower* than the risk in the United States, Canada, or northern Europe. One reason for this may be that soy isoflavones help reduce bone loss. Studies done in the United States so far have been conflicting: some studies show that soy improves bone density, and others show that it doesn't. There are some studies, like the one I cited above, that show an association between higher isoflavone levels and prevention of spinal bone loss. It should also be noted that Asian women have higher levels of phytoestrogens from childhood. This long level of exposure may help protect them from bone loss, which begins at age 30. Remember, you do not just lose bone starting at menopause. The pace of bone loss increases dramatically after menopause, but most women begin to lose bone after age 30.

There could be other factors involved in this paradox. Asian women consume more fish oil and therefore more vitamin D. They also obtain their calcium through different foods than Western women. There could be differences in the quality of calcium or vitamin D that Asian women are getting in their diet, and this may account for the decrease in bone loss among Asian women. Phytoestrogens do not reduce bone loss as well as supplemental estrogen, but as we have already discussed, the strong estrogens raise your breast cancer risk. It appears to be more beneficial to have moderate amounts of phytoestrogens over longer periods of time than to have high amounts of phytoestrogens for short periods of time. In the United States, we have the philosophy that more is better and quicker is best. Yet when we look at societies with low breast cancer levels and low osteoporosis rates, it would seem reasonable that a moderate amount of phytoestrogens consumed over longer periods of time are more protective than higher amounts used for shorter periods. This is why I want you to find good-tasting recipes for soy and flax. You need to make these a part of your everyday diet for life. The best way to do this is to find recipes that you enjoy. Obviously, if you hate what you are eating, you will not do it for long. Experiment and find those recipes you enjoy and use them.

PHYTOESTROGENS AND POSTMENOPAUSAL SYMPTOMS

Many women have noted improvement in hot flashes, night sweats, and sleep disturbances with phytoestrogen supplementation. (In the next step, we will discuss a particular phytoestrogen supplement named black cohosh.) Many of my patients have used soy and flax to control postmenopausal symptoms. By doing so, they receive many benefits.

- They reduce their symptoms, since the soy/flax isoflavones act as very weak estrogenic substances. By fitting into estrogen receptors, they mimic the effect of estrogen, but very weakly.

- They may reduce the risk of breast cancer through soy/flax's ability to improve the EQ, improve the EMI, and bind to the estrogen receptors.
- They may reduce their rate of spinal bone loss.
- They get a great-tasting source of high-quality protein. Soy seems to work better for women in perimenopause or early menopause. Yet I have seen women who are in the middle of true menopause have their symptoms controlled very nicely.

It is interesting that some Asian cultures do not have a word for menopause. This could be because Asian women are consuming so much soy isoflavones that the symptoms of menopause are relatively benign. If you can control your menopausal symptoms with soy and/or other phytoestrogens, this appears to be the safest treatment available.

Even though phytoestrogens have some very mild estrogenic activity, I have not found any studies showing an association between phytoestrogens and increased risk of breast cancer. Every study I've found has shown a correlation between phytoestrogens and *decreased* risk.

A note for women who have had breast cancer: The majority of women who have had breast cancer, particularly if it is estrogen receptor positive, have been told not to use phytoestrogen nutrients and/or supplements, for fear that mild estrogenic stimulation would cause a return of the breast cancer. This is one of those difficult questions for which there is no "right" answer for everyone. If you are menopausal and have had breast cancer, but you are miserable, cannot sleep, cannot think, and are experiencing poor sexual function, hot flashes, and night sweats, increasing the phytoestrogen foods in your diet would be a step you could discuss with your doctor.

Clinically, I have worked with many women on this very complex issue. Their quality of life is poor. They are scared to death of getting breast cancer again, and they did not tolerate or did not want to take the selected estrogen receptor modulators (tamoxifen and/or raloxifene).

I review the pros and cons of all of the therapies we discuss in this book with my patients. Of course, the final decision must be theirs, as they must accept the responsibility for their actions and their health. Many women have wished to try a middle-of-the-road approach.

They have found their quality of life to be unacceptable without any estrogen modulation. Yet, they are afraid to take an estrogen supplement, even estriol. Many of them have chosen to increase the phytoestrogens in their diet to see if it will make the symptoms more manageable while still maintaining minimal estrogenic stimulation to their breasts.

To my knowledge, no clear-cut study has been completed showing phytoestrogen either reducing or increasing the risk of *recurrent* breast cancer.

This is a study that desperately needs to be done. Unfortunately, there is very little incentive for the pharmaceutical industry or our government to proceed with that study. In any case, as I said before, never proceed with any supplementation without first consulting your physician. If you have had breast cancer, proceeding with high-dosed soy protein supplementation is *not* advised. Changes in your diet would be the first step to try to make your symptoms more manageable.

THE BOTTOM LINE

Studies have shown:

- Phytoestrogens genistein, daidzein, equol, enterolactone, and enterodiol have been associated with *reduction* in the risk of breast cancer.
- Asian populations, who consume 100 to 1,000 times the level of phytoestrogens of Western women, have a *four to seven* times lower risk of breast cancer. In studies, Asian women who were the highest 25 percent in phytoestrogen consumption had a *four times* lower risk than Asian women in the lowest 25 percent. Remember, even the Asian women in the lowest group have a four to seven times lower risk of breast cancer than you!
- Soy consumption is an excellent way to increase the phytoestrogens genistein, daidzein, and equol. Because there are still questions concerning the side effects of raw or unfermented soy products, I recommend using the fermented soy products tofu, miso, and tempeh as part of a change in your everyday diet. Your goal should be about 20 to 30 milligrams of genistein per day, which is roughly equal to 25 to 50 grams of soy protein per day.
- Ground flaxseed is an excellent source of the lignans enterodiol and enterolactone. Your goal should be 10 to 25 grams of flaxseed per day via various wholesome, great-tasting foods. At minimum, eat one flax muffin containing 10 grams of ground flaxseed daily or several times per week.

- Even if you cannot eat the recommended amount of soy and/or flax per day, do it as many times per week as possible. Consuming some soy and/or flax over the course of many months should confer some protective effect and reduce your risk of breast cancer. I want to emphasize that it is better to eat moderate amounts of soy and/or flax several times a week for years than to eat larger amounts and then burn out and quit. There are many other health benefits associated with phyton utrient consumption that we will not review in this book. These include reduction of several other types of cancer and, as I mentioned earlier, reduction in the risk of heart disease.

Consider Taking
Black Cohosh:
Nature's Symptom Fighter

Black cohosh (*Cimicifuga racemosa*) is a plant native to North America. It was used by Native Americans for a variety of ailments, including menstrual problems, arthritis, snake bites, and kidney ailments. The root of this plant contains phytoestrogens, including formononetin (an isoflavone) and 27-deoxyactein (a triterpenoid glycoside).[1]

Formononetin and 27-deoxyactein have been shown to attach to estrogen receptors. Like the isoflavones we talked about in Step 6 (soy and flax), the phytoestrogens from black cohosh have a mild estrogen-like effect.

Black cohosh has been approved by the German Ministry of Health (Kommission E) and has been one of the most prescribed herbs in Germany for several decades. For those of you who are not familiar with Kommission E, it is an FDA-like body that evaluates nutrients and supplements for effectiveness and possible toxicity. It then approves or rejects them for use by the German public.

WHAT DO THE STUDIES TELL US?

Many studies have shown black cohosh to be effective in treating the symptoms associated with menopause.

- *Study 1.* In this study, 629 women were given a liquid extract of black cohosh for 6 to 8 weeks. Eighty percent of the women had significant improvement in menopausal symptoms by the end of the study. Black cohosh was well tolerated. No one was forced to quit the study because of side effects, and only 7 percent reported stomach upset, which was resolved.[2] (To review the symptoms improved, see Table 7.1.) This study showed that nearly half of women had all their menopausal symptoms relieved.
- *Study 2.* In this study, 60 women were given either standardized black cohosh extract, Valium (2 milligrams a day), or conjugated estrogen (0.625 milligram a day) for 12 weeks. Black cohosh was shown to be more effective for the relief of depression and anxiety (associated with menopause) than either Valium or conjugated estrogen 0.625 (see Table 7.2).[3]
- *Study 3.* In this study, black cohosh was compared with conjugated estrogen (0.625 milligrams). Thirty women took black cohosh (two tablets of standardized extract twice per day), and 30 women took conjugated estrogen (0.625 milligrams daily). Black cohosh improved symptoms better than conjugated estrogen. For example, hot flashes dropped by 80 percent in the black cohosh group versus 30 percent in the conjugated estrogen group. This

Table 7.1 The Effect of Black Cohash on Menopausal Symptoms (Study 1)

Symptom	No Longer Present (%)	Improved (%)	Total Improved (%)
Hot flashes	43.3	43.3	86.6
Profuse sweating	49.9	38.6	88.5
Headache	45.7	36.2	81.9
Vertigo	51.6	35.2	86.8
Heart palpitations	54.6	35.2	90.4
Ear ringing	54.8	38.1	92.9
Nervousness/ irritability	42.4	43.2	85.6
Sleep disturbances	46.1	30.7	76.8
Depressive moods	46.0	36.5	82.5

study also showed that black cohosh was able to improve vaginal function—which included improving the elasticity of the vagina and therefore reducing pain during intercourse. The author of the study states that "black cohosh outperformed conjugated estrogen in this study."[4]

Table 7.2 Before and After Treatments

	Before	After
Black Cohosh	35	14
Conjugated estrogen	35	16
Diazepam (Valium)	35	20

Note: Numbers indicate Kupperman Index scale.

- *Study 4.* A study of 110 women compared black cohosh with a placebo. Black cohosh improved nervousness, hot flashes, and night sweats. (Women took either 2 milligrams of standardized black cohosh extract twice daily or a placebo for two months.)[5]
- *Study 5.* In this study, 60 women under the age of 40 were placed on one of four treatments. All of the women in this study were having significant menopausal symptoms. The women were divided into four groups:

   Group 1 were given black cohosh (two tablets of standarized extract twice daily).
   Group 2 were given estriol (1 milligram daily).
   Group 3 were given conjugated estrogens (1.25 milligrams daily).
   Group 4 were given estrogen and progesterone in combination (one tablet daily).

Estrogen did reduce menopausal symptoms better than the black cohosh, but the study showed that black cohosh can reduce the symptoms of menopause—and with few of the associated risks of estrogen.[6]

Discussion

These studies show that black cohosh may be able to reduce menopausal symptoms as well as or better than 0.625 milligram of conjugated estrogen, and do so safely. The most serious side effect was nausea and stomach upset for a brief time, which was easily treated. A six-month-long chronic toxicity study (in rats) was undertaken, during which the rats ingested nearly ninety times the human therapeutic dose of black cohosh. They showed no toxic effects. Black cohosh has been used by thousands of women in Germany and around the world since the 1950s. No reports of serious side effects have ever been noted. Let's discuss, however, several important precautions.

IMPORTANT DOS AND DON'TS

- *Never* use black cohosh if you are pregnant or breast-feeding. (Although it is not known if black cohosh is toxic or dangerous, no studies have been done to confirm its safety in pregnancy or breast-feeding.)
- *Never* use black cohosh if you are allergic to aspirin. Black cohosh contains salicylic acid, and you may react to this if you are allergic to aspirin.
- *Always* use a standardized extract of a brand-name black cohosh. It should be standardized to 1 milligram (or more) of triterpenes per tablet. It is vital that you use the highest quality herb and/or supplements available. The supplement industry has many ways of deceiving you. Not all products are the same. Some contain very poor quality supplements that are lower than listed in active ingredients or may contain no active ingredients whatsoever! Other products contain chemicals and/or racemic mixtures that could be harmful to your health. Remember, there is no regulatory agency monitoring the purity

of supplements. Therefore, buyer beware. Always use a brand that you know and trust. In the case of herbs, always use standardized products. Throughout this book, when I discuss nutrients and/or supplements, especially herbs, I will list for you the standardized dose and try to alert you to the most common mistakes people make when purchasing supplements.

DOSAGE

The usual dose is one to four capsules daily. The number of capsules depends on the concentration of active ingredients in each capsule. If you are taking a lower concentration (for example, 1 to 2 percent active triterpenes), then you should always start at one capsule and work up to four daily to control symptoms. If you use a stronger concentration (for example, 8 percent triterpenes), then you may only have to take one or two per day. (Triterpenes are the active ingredient in black cohosh.) As always, work with a health care provider that understands herbal therapy.

POSSIBLE SIDE EFFECTS
AND OVERDOSE

Symptoms of black cohosh overdose include headache, nausea, vomiting, dizziness, visual and nervous disturbances, breast tenderness, reduced pulse rate, and increased perspiration.[7] If you have these symptoms, reduce or discontinue black cohosh immediately.

Black cohosh has been a safe, effective therapy for controlling menopausal symptoms. It does not appear to carry the risks associated with estrogen replacement therapy (ERT) and has been used by millions of women worldwide to improve their quality of life.

No supplement, herb, or drug is without possible side effects, but black cohosh has shown a low side effect profile with minor symptoms of nausea and breast tenderness in a small percentage of the women studied (approximately 7 percent). In these studies, even the minor side effects appear to be self-limiting.

As we discussed in the last step, if you have menopausal symptoms, the place to start is with your diet. Increase the soy and flax phytoestrogens in your diet to see if you can control your symptoms. If you cannot and need a supplement to improve your quality of life, then consider standardized black cohosh in addition to your dietary changes. Use the lowest dose of black cohosh that controls your symptoms.

Through this plan, many of you will be able to avoid ERT altogether and avoid the risks associated with it. Obviously, if you are on a supplement of black cohosh, continue to get your yearly breast checks, mammograms, and Pap smears (or more frequently as advised by your personal physician). Most physicians have little knowledge of black cohosh.

Unfortunately, many physicians, instead of learning about the benefits of black cohosh, will belittle you for taking it. I never recommend hiding any supplement program from your physician. However, if your physician belittles you for taking black cohosh, then it is time to find a new physician. The days of making the patient feel foolish because the doctor is ignorant of natural or nutritional therapy are over.

THE BOTTOM LINE

- Black cohosh is a plant, the root of which contains substances that are phytoestrogens and have been used for centuries by Native Americans. It has been used as a standardized herbal therapy since the 1950s throughout Europe.
- Many studies have shown black cohosh to be as effective in relieving menopausal symptoms as low to moderate doses of conjugated estrogens.
- Studies have shown that black cohosh does not seem to increase the risk of breast cancer (unlike traditional ERT).
- While side effects are not impossible with black cohosh, they are, for the most part, rare and mild.

If your menopausal symptoms are well controlled using black cohosh as a supplement, you should work to prevent osteoporosis, since the studies are not conclusive that black cohosh protects bone.

Let's go on and talk about another hormone that is very important in reducing your breast cancer risk. This is the "Cinderella of hormones," since it is neglected by so many physicians; yet it has the power to help prevent bone loss, control many perimenopausal symptoms, and reduce your breast cancer risk. What is this "Cinderella hormone"? Progesterone.

Find Out If Progesterone Is Right for You

Progesterone is a hormone that does not receive the respect from the medical community that it is due. When you are pre-menopausal, progesterone is made in the ovaries, and your levels go up significantly the last two weeks of your cycle. If your body recognizes that you are not pregnant, progesterone levels drop dramatically, triggering your period. You make the majority of your progesterone in the last two weeks of your cycle. Progesterone goes through your bloodstream, where it exerts its effect on many organs, including the uterus, breasts, and brain, just to name a few.

HOW PROGESTERONE AFFECTS THE BODY

Most doctors forget that progesterone affects multiple organs, not just the uterus. In the brain, it has calming antidepressant-like effects and seems to help with sleep. In the breasts, it helps prevent overstimulation due to estrogen. In the skeletal system, it acts to increase bone formation, allowing a woman to actively build bone. (Remember, estrogen does not help you to build bone; it slows the breakdown of bone. This breakdown is called osteo-clastic activity.) It is important to realize that progesterone has a whole host of actions in the body beyond getting the uterus ready for conception and/or maintaining a pregnancy. In the clinic, I have seen hundreds of women who have had a total hysterectomy (ovaries and uterus removed), and they are just on estrogen replacement therapy (ERT). The gynecologists believe that because you no longer have a uterus, you no longer need progesterone. Nothing could be further from the truth!

No doubt your gynecologist is mainly thinking about your reproductive system. However, such a narrow perspective is inex-cusable. All doctors must consider the effects of their therapy on the whole body, not just one organ system. I have had many hundreds of patients find relief from their migraines, fibrocys-tic breasts, and anxiety and experience improvement of their libido once they started on natural bioidentical progesterone. The crazy thing about it is that many of these patients had gone to their gynecologist, prior to seeing me, complaining of these exact symp-toms. They were told they were depressed and were prescribed an antidepressant! Unfortunately, ignorance is not bliss when it is *your* body that has to go without progesterone. If you have had a total hysterectomy, you still need *progesterone*! (For the type and dose, see the end of this step.)

In addition, I have seen many symptomatic women (with intact ovaries) in their thirties or early forties who are not low in estro-gen, but are low in progesterone. There are several reasons for this.

By the age of 35, approximately 50 percent of women have dys-functional follicles leading to cycles where they do not ovulate[1] and therefore do not produce much progesterone. If you are one of these women who either do not ovulate or ovulate irregularly, you may be low in progesterone and suffer from the associated symptoms.

Stress is another important factor. In times of high stress, the body is able to take progesterone and remove one small side group to make it into cortisone. When you are under stress, cortisone becomes the more important hormone. You need higher levels of cortisone to handle either psychological or physical stress. If the stress continues for a prolonged period of time, progesterone levels start to go down, causing symptoms. This has one evolutionary advantage in that if your progesterone levels drop significantly, you will not make the progesterone necessary to maintain a pregnancy. Think about this for a minute. In the not-so-distant past, prolonged stress was from war, famine, or severe prolonged weather changes. This is not exactly a great time to have a baby, so the body accomplishes two goals with one process. You get more cortisone (which you need in times of stress) and it becomes harder for you to become pregnant (which you do not need during war or famine).

Let's look at what happens in the twenty-first century. Stresses are no longer war, famine, or disease (at least not for most of us in the Western world). More than likely, your stresses are job stresses, marital problems, law suits, traffic jams, and financial problems, just to name a few. Some of you may stay under severe stress for many years. These stresses last for decades and slowly wear down your adrenal glands. The adrenal glands are small glands at the top of your kidneys where you make over 100 hormones, including cortisone and DHEA. After menopause, these glands are responsible for making estrogen and progesterone, since your ovaries are no longer functioning or are functioning in a reduced capacity. If you wear down your adrenals by living a stressed life, you are no longer able to produce the cortisone necessary to handle stress. Your body then pulls progesterone into the cortisol pathway to try to compensate, and you are left with chronically low progesterone levels (this assumes that your ovaries are functioning properly). This is a big assumption, since most women who have worn-down adrenal function also have ovarian dysfunction.

Many of you reading this right now are low in progesterone, since it is the most common sex hormone deficiency in a premenopausal woman. Symptoms of progesterone deficiency can include irregular periods, fibrocystic breast disease, anxiety, depression, mood swings (particularly prior to menses), difficulty thinking, and more.

WHAT DOES ALL THIS HAVE TO DO WITH BREAST CANCER?

Progesterone is vital to balancing the stimulatory effects of estrogen in the breasts. We have already talked at length about how estrogen (with the exception of estriol) strongly stimulates breast tissue cellular reproduction. The higher your strong estrogen levels, the more rapidly your breast tissue will reproduce and the thicker and larger your breasts become, eventually developing fibrocysts. If this cellular reproduction is not controlled, you could develop a tumor (that is, cancer). At the same time, we have discussed the fact that estrogen is vital in keeping your breast tissue young, firm, and healthy (among its many other benefits). *The key is balance!* Progesterone was designed to balance out the stimulatory effects of estrogen in the breast and elsewhere.

Progesterone does so through at least two mechanisms. The first is that progesterone decreases cell division in the breast.[2] A study was done where women about to undergo biopsy for what turned out to be benign lumps were given either estrogen or progesterone, and the removed tissue was examined for how actively the cells were reproducing. The estrogen caused an increase in breast tissue reproduction (as expected), while the progesterone caused a significant decrease in cell reproduction.[3]

Other studies done with progestins did not show the same protective effect. Progestins are synthetic substances that resemble progesterone but are not true progesterone. Progestins sometimes act like progesterone, but because they do not have the identical chemical structure of human progesterone, they can have unintended side effects. Progestins were developed in the 1960s before we knew that hormones are very specific messengers with very specific structures and if you alter that structure, you may alter function or increase side effects. (Progestins are not true progesterone; that is why, as we will discuss later, you should only use bioidentical progesterone.) This may be why the progestins in the Women's Health Initiative (WHI) study increased breast cancer risk, whereas many studies show that bioidentical progesterone does not appear to increase risk. The second mechanism is that progesterone reduces the conversion of estrogen to the most dangerous metabolite, the 4 OH form.[4] The 4 OH metabolite has been associated with increased breast cancer risk.

Research has shown that women who are low in progesterone are at a greater risk of breast cancer and are twice as likely to die of that breast cancer as a woman with normal progesterone levels.[5] This study published in the *American Journal of Epidemiology* in 1981 also showed that women who were deficient in progesterone were over *five times* as likely to get breast cancer as those with normal progesterone levels.[6]

A 1998 study published in the *Annals of Clinical and Laboratory Science* found that the function of a tumor suppressor gene (p53) was improved by progesterone.[7] (If the function of your tumor suppressor genes improves, your breast cancer risk goes down.)

HOW DO WE MEASURE PROGESTERONE LEVELS?

The best way to measure progesterone is through saliva. We are measuring free progesterone levels, and it is this free hormone that has the ability to exert its effect. Salivary measurements are an excellent way of measuring nearly all hormones, since it gives the free hormone levels, which, as stated above, are the hormones that are active. Many hormones are protein bound or bound to binding substances such as SHBG (sex hormone binding globulin), which binds estrogen and/or progesterone and does not allow the hormone to exert its effects on other parts of the body. In addition, analyzing saliva is easy, so it allows us to obtain levels at several different times during the cycle, improving accuracy. Remember, you make the majority of progesterone the last two weeks of your cycle. This is when progesterone should be measured. Millions of you have had serum progesterone levels measured and were told that your progesterone levels were "normal." Serum progesterone, however, evaluates the bound and unbound hormone (total progesterone) and does not give an accurate reflection of your free hormone status. If your doctor does a serum progesterone level, make sure he or she also orders a *free* progesterone level and that it is done during the eighteenth to twenty-first day of your cycle.

WHAT TYPE OF
PROGESTERONE SUPPLEMENTATION IS BEST?

Always use natural bioidentical progesterone. Most doctors prescribe synthetic progestins, which are not true progesterones. Progestins are progesterone-like hormones that exert progesterone-*like* effects in *some instances*, but in other instances have effects different from progesterone's. One of the problems has been that progesterone is a natural substance and cannot be patented; therefore, a pharmaceutical company cannot hold the unchallenged patent on bioidentical progesterone. For this reason, pharmaceutical companies developed progestins, which are substances that mimic progesterone but are not the same hormone. Studies now are showing that progestins may increase the risk of breast cancer. These studies include the WHI, which showed that women on a conjugated estrogen/synthetic progestin had a significant increase in their risk of breast cancer. Your doctor, including most gynecologists, may not be familiar with natural progesterone. One piece of good news is that oral progesterone has been released by a major pharmaceutical company in tablet form. Therefore, many physicians are becoming familiar with progesterone through that pharmaceutical company. The problem is that you should never take oral progesterone unless absolutely necessary. Similar to the situation with estrogen, progesterone cream is well absorbed; therefore, you are able to use lower doses than with oral progesterone. Oral progesterone has to be given in much higher doses, with a large percentage of it being converted to metabolites.

Progesterone Cream

If you are going to take progesterone, make sure it is natural, bioidentical progesterone, and make sure it is progesterone cream. Progesterone creams should be made by a competent compounding pharmacist. Many creams are in a soy base. If you are allergic to soy, then creams are available in a nonsoy formula.

You may consider a low dose, 12.5 milligrams or possibly less, and titrate up if you do not get relief from your symptoms. For a premenopausal woman with intact ovaries and uterus, we give progesterone cream the last two weeks of the cycle to more closely mimic what she would produce naturally. The doses can range between 6 and 100 milligrams (average dose is 12.5 to 25 milligrams). The higher doses are usually reserved for those women with very severe PMS. If you are a postmenopausal woman, you need lower amounts of progesterone to mimic what the body would normally produce after menopause. You can take progesterone daily, in smaller amounts (usually 6 to 25 milligrams). As I discussed in Step 3, if you are on estriol cream, progesterone can be built into the same cream. This will reduce your cost and also reduce the hassle.

POSSIBLE SIDE EFFECTS

The major side effect from progesterone, if you have an intact uterus and take too much progesterone, is early or prolonged menstrual bleeding (bleeding between periods). If this happens, slowly reduce the dose of progesterone to eliminate that side effect. Most women also find progesterone helpful for fibrocystic disease. I have had only one or two patients who felt that it increased their fibrocystic tenderness, and they discontinued the progesterone.

THE BOTTOM LINE

Progesterone is the "Cinderella of hormones," as it has too often been ignored or misunderstood. We have briefly reviewed some of the evidence showing that progesterone appears to be important in preventing breast cancer. The study published in the *American Journal of Epidemiology* showed that women who were deficient in progesterone were five times as likely to get breast cancer as women who were not deficient in progesterone. Not only is progesterone protective for the breasts, but it has therapeutic effects throughout the body, including stabilizing and calming the nervous system, encouraging bone production, protecting and/or encouraging thyroid function, and boosting energy production. Millions of you who have had a total hysterectomy have been told you have no need for progesterone. I hope you see by now that nothing could be further from the truth. If your progesterone levels are low (and since your ovaries have been removed, we assume your levels are low), you should consider progesterone supplementation. For those of you with many of the symptoms we have discussed, get a free progesterone level near the twenty-first day of your cycle (day 1 is the first day of your flow) to determine if progesterone may be helpful for you.

Get More of the Super Vitamin E to Reduce Your Breast Cancer Risk

Vitamin E is one of the most important fat-soluble antioxidants in our body. Because breasts are predominantly fat, it would make sense that vitamin E could reduce oxidative damage to breast tissue, therefore reducing the risk of breast cancer. But is this true? Do medical studies support the idea that vitamin E reduces breast cancer risks? Let's look at the studies.

WHAT DO THE STUDIES TELL US?

An interesting observation has been made over the last several years. Studies of women who eat foods high in vitamin E suggest that these women have a significant reduction in their breast cancer risk, yet women taking vitamin E supplements, sometimes at several hundred times the dose that you would get from your diet, did not reduce their risk of cancer at all.[1,2] What's going on here? To answer that, let's first review the results of a study on total vitamin E intake (from food) and reduction of breast cancer risks, since that study is rather compelling.

- If you were premenopausal with a family history of breast cancer and you were in the group of women with the highest vitamin E levels, you had a *90 percent reduction of your risk of breast cancer.*
- If you were a premenopausal woman without a family history of breast cancer and were in the group with the highest levels of vitamin E, you had a *50 percent risk reduction.*
- If you were a postmenopausal woman without a family history of breast cancer and you were in the group that is highest in vitamin E, you had a *50 percent reduction of breast cancer risk.*
- Lastly, if you were a postmenopausal woman with a family history of breast cancer and you were in the group highest in vitamin E, you still had a *30 percent reduction of breast cancer risk.*[3]

This remarkable study shows that if you obtain high levels of vitamin E at a younger age, you may achieve a 90 percent reduction in your breast cancer risk, even if you have a positive family history. This is just with vitamin E alone, not including all of the other risk-reducing secrets we have discussed! Importantly, it also shows that it is never too late, since even postmenopausal women had a 30 to 50 percent reduction in their breast cancer risk with high levels of vitamin E. This study is truly amazing! Note, however, that all the vitamin E in this study came from *dietary sources.* Studies done on alpha-tocopherol (the type of vitamin E usually found in Vitamin E supplements) are much less compelling. In fact, many of these studies failed to show significant risk reduction at all with vitamin E supplementation.[4]

How can this be? It is important to remember that vitamin E is not just one vitamin; it is a *family* made up of many different members. Alpha-tocopherol was the first member of the vitamin E family discovered and was therefore given the name vitamin E. For many decades, doctors thought it was that simple: vitamin E was alpha-tocopherol. What they did not know and what we know now is that there is not only alpha-tocopherol, but also beta-, delta-, and gamma-tocopherol. All of these tocopherols, plus the tocotrienols (beta, delta, and gamma) together make up what we now know as vitamin E. These substances work as a team and occur together in nature in the same foods. That is why when you take commercially available vitamin E supplements, in most cases you are getting just a small fraction of the true benefits of vitamin E complex. It's like a football coach hiring a quarterback but not bothering to hire any blockers or receivers. It's nice to have a quarterback, but without other qualified team members, you're not getting the maximal result. The same principle applies with vitamin E. You need the whole team to get the true benefits from vitamin E.

Let's talk for a few minutes about the vitamin E cousins named tocotrienols. I hope you will be as impressed with this information as I was when I first reviewed it.

In several studies, tocotrienols were shown to slow the growth of estrogen receptor positive breast cancer cells (in a laboratory culture) by up to 50 percent.[5] Some studies have shown that tocotrienols also work on estrogen receptor negative (ER negative) breast cancer. Tocotrienols appear to slow the growth of breast cancer cells by restoring their ability to self-destruct.[6] All cells have a mechanism that allows them to self-destruct if they become too damaged or abnormal. However, this mechanism is lacking in cancer cells. Cancer cells, even though they are very abnormal, continue to reproduce, eventually building up enough numbers to cause a tumor. If this self-destructive mechanism was maintained, as it is in normal cells, then the cells would detect that they had become significantly abnormal and self-destruct. Tocotrienols help to restore the self-destructing mechanisms of breast cancer cells.

It is not surprising that studies have shown that regular vitamin E supplements (alpha-tocopherol) do not appear to reduce the risk of breast cancer, while other members of the vitamin E family, including the "cousins" named tocotrienols, may significantly reduce the risk of breast cancer and restore breast cancer cells' ability to self-destruct. This is why the studies showed that the vitamin E obtained from the diet significantly reduced the risk of breast cancer in premenopausal and postmenopausal women alike. The vitamin E obtained from the diet is the complete vitamin E complex found in foods.

VITAMIN E AND THE AMERICAN DIET

It is interesting to note that the Standard American Diet (SAD) contains very little vitamin E. Most vitamin E occurs in whole grains, particularly the germ of the grain. The germ is the part of the grain that can sprout, with the remainder of the kernel being mostly starch to feed the new sprout once it develops. The germ is the part of the kernel, be it wheat, corn, or any other grain, that is also highest in oil. As you know, oil can turn rancid if left on the shelf for long periods of time. Beginning roughly in the mid-twentieth century, food companies figured out that if they removed the germ from the grain, the bread would last much longer on the shelf. Prior to that, most breads were made with whole grain and once baked would last only for several days. Many of you remember, as I do, day-old bread being sold at half price at the local bakery. Bread containing the whole grain, including the germ, spoiled more quickly than bread where the germ had been removed and preservatives added. As a poor college student, I once kept a loaf of bread on my shelf for two months without it spoiling! (The name of this bread is being withheld to protect the not so innocent.)

Food companies removed the germ and replaced it with the newly discovered vitamin E, thinking they were replacing some of the same nutrients that they had removed. Remember, this vitamin E was just alpha-tocopherol, since no one knew that vitamin E was an entire family. They call this bread enriched! As my father used to say, "That is like taking a dollar from you, giving you 7 cents back, and telling you that you're enriched!" Another interesting tidbit from my father: When mice get into the corn crib and can eat any part of the corn they please, all they eat is the germ. They leave the remainder of the kernel, the part that contains mostly starch. Do you think nature is trying to tell us something? If mice know enough to eat just the germ and you are many times smarter than a mouse, then what is your excuse for eating the part of the kernel that even a mouse doesn't want? And this is not just true for corn; wheat, rice, and all grains have had the germ removed unless they are "whole." When you eat white rice, the rice bran and germ have been removed; therefore, very little vitamin E or tocotrienol remains. To get the true benefit from rice, you need to eat natural whole rice.

The mice seem to know instinctively what's good for them— the germ that contains the majority of nutrients, oils, and antioxidants that are so important for health. In addition, the mice do not have food companies preparing their foods, nor do they have to watch the endless stream of TV advertisements selling foods that are not very beneficial to their health. Tocotrienol supplements are usually made from rice bran or palm oil. Because tocotrienols are fat soluble, they tend to be concentrated in your breast tissue (which is mostly fat). And since these vitamin E family members are fat soluble, they don't wash out of the body as easily as water-soluble vitamins. Therefore, eating small amounts of foods containing the vitamin E family every day may pay big benefits (see Table 9.1).

WHAT ABOUT SUPPLEMENTS?

If you want to use a supplement, what should you look for?

- Never take a vitamin E that is just alpha-tocopherol.
- Always supplement with a vitamin E that contains the whole family—mixed tocopherols plus tocotrienols.
- You *can* overdose on vitamin E because it is fat soluble, but you have to try pretty hard. Several studies have shown that 240 milligrams per day of tocotrienols for 16 months produce no adverse side effects.[7] One study also showed that supplementation of 78 milligrams of tocotrienols for 1 month produced an eightfold increase of tocotrienols in blood levels. These blood levels approximated the level that was found to slow estrogen receptor positive breast cancer cell division by 50 percent.[8]

Table 9.1 Foods High in Vitamin E

Foods	Milligrams Vitamin E
Wheat germ,* 2 tablespoons	20.0
Almonds, 1 ounce	7.5
Whole grain bread, 1 slice	1–3.0
Rice bran, 100 grams	45.0
Mango (½ cup sliced, raw)	2.3
Hazelnuts (dry roasted 1 ounce)	4.5
Sunflower seeds, 2 tablespoons	10.0
Shrimp, 3 ounces	5–7.0 (approx.)
Broccoli, (½ cup, frozen)	1.5
Spinach, ½ cup	1.0 (approx.)

Source: National Institute of Health, Office of Dietary Supplements

*Here's an easy tip to increase the vitamin E in your diet. Add 2 tablespoons of organic wheat germ to your favorite cereal (hot or cold), or add it to your flax muffin recipe. Wheat allergy is the third most common allergy in the United States, so avoid wheat germ if you suspect you are allergic to wheat.

- Other studies have shown gamma-tocopherol and possibly tocotrienols to be COX-2 inhibitors.[9] COX-2 enzyme has been implicated in the development of cancer. As we will discuss in later steps, inhibition or reduction of the COX-2 enzyme reduces your cancer risk.

OTHER BENEFITS OF VITAMIN E

We have kept our discussion of vitamin E restricted to its benefits in reducing breast cancer. Of course, you have fat in many other areas of your body, and the benefits from mixed vitamin E supplementation may include: cardiovascular risk reduction, reduction in inflammation, slowing of the aging process, and reduced risk of several other cancers. This is one of those simple secrets you can use to dramatically reduce your risk of breast cancer! The information that we have reviewed concerning tocotrienols is truly cutting-edge. You may not read about it in newspapers or the popular press for years. Your doctor may not know about it for decades. You now have this dramatic information that you can use to significantly reduce your breast cancer risk. Vitamin E complex supplementation is part of an overall breast cancer reduction plan that can dramatically reduce the chances of you ever hearing those dreaded words, "You have breast cancer."

IMPORTANT NOTE ABOUT
VITAMIN E AND HEART DISEASE

A study published in 2005 in the *Annals of Internal Medicine* has received a large amount of publicity. This study found that people taking 200 IU (international units) or less of vitamin E a day were less likely to die of heart disease than those taking more. Of course, many doctors were quick to jump on this and recommend that their patients reduce or (worse yet) stop their vitamin E supplements. This study, however, had at least two flaws:

1. It studied people taking alpha-tocopherol; and remember that the other members of the tocopherol family have a more beneficial effect on cancer prevention and prevention of heart disease.
2. The researchers did not sort out why people were taking higher-dose vitamin E in the first place. Many people begin taking vitamin E when they find out they had heart problems; having prior heart disease would of course leave these people at higher risk of death from heart disease.

The long and short of it is that many studies have found the vitamin E family to be beneficial in breast cancer avoidance and helpful in prevention of heart disease as well! Just remember: If you take a vitamin E supplement, take one that contains the whole "family" and don't overdo it, since vitamin E can be stored in the body. Unfortunately, the *Annals of Internal Medicine* study, in my opinion, will end up harming people, since I am sure many thousands will avoid vitamin E supplementation in the future

THE BOTTOM LINE

- High dietary vitamin E has been shown to reduce the risk of breast cancer from 50 to 90 percent in premenopausal women and 30 to 50 percent in postmenopausal women.
- The vitamin E family consists of many members, not just alpha-tocopherol. Alpha-tocopherol is the type of vitamin E that is in most commercial vitamin E supplements.

- You should immediately increase the foods that are high in vitamin E content (see Table 9.1 on page 102).
- Supplementation of a complete vitamin E complex makes sense for most women. As we have discussed, make sure your supplement contains mixed tocopherols plus tocotrienols. But be careful. Some supplements will say "with mixed tocopherols," but when you read the label, only a small fraction of the total E is beta, delta, and gamma. Your dose should be 100 to 400 IU daily.
- Vitamin E supplements should be taken with meals, since they are oil based and require some fat in our food to be effectively absorbed.
- If you are on blood-thinning medications, such as warfarin (Coumadin) or heparin, vitamin E may increase the thinning effect. *Always* consult with your physician prior to starting vitamin E supplementation if you are on blood-thinning medications. Vitamin E may be very beneficial for cardiovascular disease. In most cases, people on blood-thinning medications can take a vitamin E supplement as long as their medication levels are monitored and the dose adjusted as needed.

Discover Curcumin: Nature's Anticancer Secret Agent

Curcumin is the active ingredient in turmeric. Turmeric is a relative of ginger and has a deep yellow-orange color, which contains antioxidants. Turmeric has been used in the ancient medicines of India and China for nearly 4,000 years. Many ancient texts have described the anti-inflammatory properties of turmeric. It has been used for the treatment of various diseases, including arthritis and bowel dysfunction. Turmeric is probably one of those substances that began as a medicine and eventually evolved into a ubiquitous part of the culture's diet. As a result, many recipes from India contain turmeric. Not only does it taste great; it also serves as an anti-inflammatory medication!

HOW DOES CURCUMIN PROTECT BREAST CELLS?

Curcumin can block chemicals like DDT and dioxin from getting inside your breast cells. It does this by attaching itself to the "Ah" receptor. This is the receptor that DDT and dioxin use to gain access to your breast cells, causing harm. (Remember, we discussed the "Ah" receptor in Step 5; there we saw that I3C and DIM also can keep dioxin and DDT from attaching to the "Ah" receptor and triggering uncontrollable breast cell reproduction.) In one study, the presence of curcumin in the body reduced DDT's ability to cause growth of breast cancer by 75 percent.[1] Another study showed that curcumin reduced the growth of estrogen-sensitive breast cancer cells by 98 percent![2]

Curcumin helps protect your breast cells from several types of damage, including harmful chemicals and radiation. Rats irradiated to produce breast cancer were given curcumin. The group given the curcumin had one-quarter the risk of developing breast cancer as those rats that did not receive curcumin.[3] Another study confirmed the amazing finding that 8 out of 10 irradiated rats got breast cancer versus 3 out of 10 for the group that received curcumin and radiation at the same time![4]

How can curcumin have such a dramatic protective effect on breast cells and such a devastating effect on breast cancer?

- Curcumin appears to block breast cancer growth factors. It interferes with those growth signals that breast cancer cells produce, therefore slowing breast cancer growth rates. Studies have shown that curcumin inhibits several types of these growth factors, and this may be why curcumin has been found to be helpful in preventing multiple known cancers.[5]
- Curcumin also causes cancer cells to self-destruct. In the last step (on vitamin E), we discussed that when cells become abnormal or damaged, they usually trigger a self-destruction mechanism. This is known as *apoptosis.*

This is one way the body keeps control over damaged cells, stopping them from reproducing. Cancer cells are able to short-circuit apoptosis, continuing to reproduce until they become a dangerous tumor. Curcumin, like vitamin E, seems to restore a cell's ability to recognize that it is damaged, therefore triggering the self-destruct mechanism.[6] At this time, although it is unknown exactly what mechanism or quality of curcumin allows it to improve apoptosis, we know that curcumin is a very powerful antioxidant and it may be through this strong antioxidant activity that it improves apoptosis.

- Curcumin slows the growth of cancer cells in the early stage of the disease[7]—a stage where cancer cells are moderately different from the cells around them. This is one reason why it has an effect on cancer cells yet does not harm normal cells.

- Curcumin appears to fight breast cancer by improving immunity. This is not surprising, since curcumin is known to be a strong anti-inflammatory and antioxidant. In one study, animals that were given curcumin had increased levels of cancer-fighting immune factors.[8]

- Curcumin also appears to inhibit substances that cause tumors to grow blood vessels. Tumors require more blood than normal cells because of their rapid growth.[9] Without the proper blood supply, tumors simply cannot continue to grow; therefore, slowing of blood vessel growth is an important factor in controlling the growth rate of the tumor and your survival. Currently, pharmaceutical companies are actively working at finding substances that can slow the growth of blood vessels into a cancer. There is a lot of money to be made from finding a synthetic substance that can treat cancer in this way. The neat thing for us is that nature has provided an anticancer substance that has been known for roughly 4,000 years and that we can use to slow the growth of breast cancer or prevent it in the first place—curcumin! Very few side effects have been associated with curcumin. It appears to be a very safe, natural spice/medicine/supplement. A test done at M. D Anderson Cancer Center in Houston (2005) showed that curcumin slowed the spread of breast cancer in mice, better than the anti-cancer drug Taxol. Half of the mice that received curcumin had spread of breast cancer to the lungs versus 95 percent of the mice that received placebo (75 percent of the mice that were given Taxol alone had cancer spread to the lungs). Importantly, only 25 percent of mice that got both curcumin and Taxol had cancer spread to the lungs. This shows that not only is curcumin powerful in its own right but that when used in combination with anti-cancer drugs it may improve the effectiveness of those drugs.[10]

THE BOTTOM LINE

- Curcumin is a strong antioxidant, which allows it to protect breast cells from oxidative damage.
- It binds to the "Ah" receptor, blocking the overstimulatory effects of cancer-causing chemicals.

- It helps cancer cells recognize the fact that they are growing out of control and reestablishes the self-destruct signal, causing the defective cells to self-destruct before they develop into a tumor.
- It appears to improve immunity through improving several immune factors. By improving your immune factors, you improve the chances of your immune system recognizing and destroying cancer cells *before* they go out of control.
- Curcumin is an excellent anti-inflammatory via its reduction of the COX-2 enzyme. It appears to reduce many types of inflammation, including the types of inflammation that can lead to cancer.
- Lastly, it reduces the growth of blood vessels into tumor cells, thereby depriving those cells of the nutrients they need to continue to reproduce.

Make the Most of Melatonin: Nature's Cancer-Preventing Hormone

Scientists have been both puzzled and fascinated by a study published in the journal *Epidemiology* in May 1991. This study showed that blind women had a lower risk of breast cancer than women who maintained their sight.[1] What in the world can explain this phenomenon?

Was genetics the answer? It doesn't seem likely, since this study included not only women who were blind from birth, but also women blinded as a result of accidents. Was it diet? No, since these women appeared to have the same diet as women who could see. Another study came out in 2001, reported in the *British Journal of Cancer*.

In that study, the researchers evaluated 15,000 women who were visually impaired. It was found that the blind women had a 36 percent *lower* risk of breast cancer than women with normal sight.[2] How did the researchers explain this? What does a blind woman have that a woman with sight does not? The answer is that a blind woman has higher levels of the hormone melatonin.

WHAT IS MELATONIN AND HOW DOES IT WORK?

Melatonin is a hormone produced in a small gland of the brain named the pineal. We make melatonin from the amino acid tryptophan via the process outlined below.

Sunlight
Tryptophan → 5-hydroxytryptophan (5-HTP)

Darkness
Serotonin → Melatonin

Besides the appropriate enzymes, the other vital ingredient needed to make melatonin is darkness. The blind women had significantly higher levels of melatonin because they were in darkness or near darkness 24 hours a day (they could see very little light). Darkness enhances the production of melatonin.

The precursor of melatonin, the amino acid tryptophan, is found in turkey, chicken, milk, tuna, and soy. It is converted via enzymatic processes to the hormone serotonin, which is associated with improved mood, elevated alertness, and excitement. When the sun goes down and we are exposed to darkness, serotonin is converted to melatonin. Melatonin is associated with calmness and sleep. One factor that decreases melatonin is exposure to light in the evening. We will discuss this factor later in this step.

The big question is, Why does melatonin so dramatically reduce the risk of breast cancer? The answer may lie in the fact that melatonin is a very powerful antioxidant. In fact, melatonin may be the most potent antioxidant in your body! Another important factor is that it crosses all known membranes. Therefore, melatonin is both fat and water soluble and able to travel to all cells of the body. When we are young, we can make melatonin exceptionally well. (Ever notice how a 5-year-old seems to be able to fall asleep instantly?)

As we age, our ability to make melatonin declines. By age 65, we make only 20 to 25 percent of the amount of melatonin we made when we were 21. The decrease in melatonin production seems to begin around age 40 and escalates with age. No one totally understands why melatonin production begins to slow once we reach 40. One reason could be that through the years, the enzymes that help us make melatonin have become damaged; therefore, we have trouble converting tryptophan to melatonin. Another reason could be nutritional deficiency—especially with regard to tryptophan. At the clinic, we did an unpublished study that showed that 80 percent of the patients tested were deficient in tryptophan.[3] The cause of this tryptophan deficiency was twofold:

1. As we age, our milk consumption tends to decline; therefore, we get less tryptophan, since milk products are excellent sources of tryptophan.
2. A large percentage of people over age 40 have low stomach acid. As we saw before, many doctors and advertisements would have us believe that we have too much stomach acid, but the truth is that many of us have too little! The amino acid tryptophan requires normal stomach acid levels to be absorbed. If your stomach acid is low, you cannot absorb tryptophan properly, even if you are getting tryptophan in your diet. As we have discussed before, millions of people

are taking acid-suppressive medications. These medications reduce the stomach acid, increase the pH of your stomach, and may reduce tryptophan absorption.

Less tryptophan means less serotonin, and less serotonin means less melatonin. This may be one reason so many people in the Western world are depressed. Serotonin is an important antidepression brain chemical, and melatonin is a vital hormone that improves both quantity and quality of sleep.

HOW SLEEP AFFECTS MELATONIN PRODUCTION

A couple of studies point to the connection between sleep patterns and melatonin production. The first study is from the *Journal of the National Cancer Institute*, which did an analysis of 78,000 women taking part in the Nurses Health Study. The analysis showed that "women who worked up to 29 years on a rotating night shift experienced a moderate increase in breast cancer. Those women who worked over 30 years on rotating night shifts had a *36 percent increase* in their breast cancer risk."[4] The other study, published again in the *Journal of the National Cancer Institute,* showed that women who did not sleep from 1 A.M. to 2 A.M. had an elevated risk of breast cancer.[5] These studies suggest that one reason for the increased risk is the lower levels of melatonin. Even though a woman on a third shift will make some melatonin during the day while she is asleep, she never really produces the amounts that would be expected from someone who sleeps at night. The second study confirms what has been known about melatonin production: we seem to make most of our melatonin between 1 A.M. and 2 A.M. If you are not asleep at 1 A.M. you lose a significant amount of your melatonin production, even if you still get a full 8 hours sleep. This reduction in melatonin contributes to poor-quality sleep, reduced immunity, and reduced antioxidant function. Any of these effects or a combination of the above can contribute to increased breast cancer risk.

WHAT YOU CAN DO TO IMPROVE MELATONIN PRODUCTION AND DECREASE YOUR BREAST CANCER RISK

Giving up your sight to prevent breast cancer seems a little drastic. Let's review what else you can do to improve your levels of melatonin.

- Make sure you are asleep before 1 A.M.
- Eat foods that are high in tryptophan. (That is why your grandmother said to have a glass of warm milk at bedtime. She did not know the medical reasons; she just knew that warm milk helped you to fall asleep. That's because of the amino acid tryptophan.) Millions of you are allergic to milk. If you are, you can use soy products and increase your consumption of turkey, preferably at supper. Because turkey is high in tryptophan, it can cause drowsiness. (That's why we fall asleep in the living room after Thanksgiving dinner!) Therefore, it is best to eat turkey in the evening.

- If you are on acid-suppressive medications, see if you can eliminate your food allergies. This may allow you to reduce the amount of medication or take it less often. This reduction in acid-suppressive medication may enhance your absorption of tryptophan. (*Caution:* Always consult with your health care practitioner before altering your medication.)
- Touching, hugging, and sex all increase melatonin production. This is one of those natural therapies that is not only good for you but can be fun. (Let's face it, sex is more fun than taking a melatonin pill!)
- Make sure you turn down your lights, especially after 10 P.M. Millions of you sit all evening with every light in the house turned on, watching TV or using the computer until bedtime. You then turn off the lights and the TV and expect to go to sleep. Remember, your brain takes several hours to make enough melatonin to allow for optimal quality and quantity of sleep. Dim down the lights after 9 or 10 P.M.

  Try not to watch TV or use the computer after 10 P.M. If you get up at night, have a very low intensity night light in the bathroom or use a weak penlight. Studies have shown that even a quick 1-second flash of light can disrupt melatonin production. If a loved one must read in bed, have the individual use a book light. That way the remainder of the lights in the bedroom can be turned off. If your bedroom is bright at night, either from security lighting or street lights, buy some black-out curtains. The more light in your bedroom at night, the lower your melatonin production.

WHAT ABOUT SUPPLEMENTS?

If none of the previous suggestions provides you with the right amount of melatonin, you can also purchase melatonin supplements at health stores. Millions of Americans over age 40 use them to fall asleep. If you are under age 40, it is best to use melatonin intermittently. The exception to this is people with chronic illnesses. A chronic illness may disrupt your ability to make melatonin; therefore, melatonin supplements may be helpful under those circumstances for people younger than 40. Use the lowest dose that helps you fall asleep. Begin at 1 milligram or less sublingual (under the tongue) if possible. You can always increase the dose if you need to. Like any hormone, melatonin works on a feedback mechanism. This means that if you take large amounts of supplemental melatonin, it could inhibit your brain's production of intrinsic melatonin.

We have discussed the quality of supplements several times, I know. But there is a lot of poor-quality melatonin available. If you are going to take a melatonin supplement, make sure it says on the bottle that it is assayed by the HPLC method (the HPLC method is the best method for determining purity of melatonin). Also, if you have an autoimmune disorder, use melatonin only under the direct supervision of a knowledgeable health care practitioner. Melatonin improves immunity, and if you have an autoimmune disorder, you may not want to upregulate your immune system further. And never use melatonin if you are pregnant or breast-feeding.

Your doctor may not be aware of the scientific studies showing melatonin's effectiveness. Always consult a health care practitioner who has used and *understands* melatonin's risks and benefits prior to using melatonin long term.

THE BOTTOM LINE

In this step, we have shown that melatonin may reduce breast cancer risk by as much as 36 percent. We learned that it probably does this through its antioxidant effects, its ability to boost immunity, and its improvement of sleep. You learned that many of you are not able to make normal amounts of melatonin owing to sleep disturbances, nutritional deficiencies, or your own bad habits. Improving your level of melatonin is a vital part of your complete breast cancer prevention strategy.

Let's continue now and review several other natural nutrients that may play an important role in reducing your breast cancer risk by 90 percent or more!

Reduce Your Risk with Other Nutrients

In addition to the ones already mentioned, there are several other nutrients and antioxidants that may greatly reduce your risk of developing breast cancer.

WHAT ARE ANTIOXIDANTS?

Oxidation is the damage process of nature. Under a variety of circumstances, our bodies create "free radicals." These free radicals are electrons, and if not neutralized, they will slam into DNA and other important cellular structures, causing damage. Antioxidants function to absorb these free radicals *before* they damage us! The more free radicals you generate, the more antioxidants you require. We generate free radicals through a variety of activities. The process of making energy itself generates free radicals. (We convert our food to chemical energy inside small power plants called *mitochondria*, located inside every cell. This conversion of food to the chemical energy ATP produces free radicals as a by-product.)

We require large amounts of antioxidants every day just to quench the free radicals we generate when we make our energy.

Then we do stupid things to generate even more free radicals. Some damage is due to free radical generation from the sun striking our skin or our eyes. Cigarettes damage our tissue through the generation of free radicals, which over the years causes disruption and damage to the DNA of various organs, including the breasts, and eventually results in cancer. Excessive use of alcohol, certain medications, and long-term stress all generate large amounts of free radials. The more free radicals we generate, the more antioxidants we use up. If we do not get sufficient antioxidants in our diet, over time we go "bankrupt"—that is, we generate more free radicals than we have antioxidants to quench them. That is when the free radical damage really starts to pile up. Just like a boxer whose arms are down, we start to get pummeled. Eventually, more damage is done to our DNA than we can repair. Cells start to reproduce wildly because of this damaged DNA. These wildly reproducing cells eventually become a tumor.

Fruits and vegetables have antioxidants because they need to protect themselves from the sun. Plants must have sunlight to generate energy, yet even for plants this is a double-edged sword, since sunlight also can cause free radical damage. The goal for the plant is to use the sunlight for energy yet avoid the damage. The color pigments in fruits and vegetables—lutein in spinach, lycopene in tomatoes, carotene in squash or carrots, flavonoids in blueberries and cherries—all have been developed by the plant to protect itself from sun damage.

All animals have developed, over time, an ability to use plant-based antioxidants to protect themselves from free radical damage. We, of course, can make certain antioxidants in our bodies. These include substances like glutathione, which is an important antioxidant we make from three separate amino acids.

Other antioxidants, however, we must obtain through diet. An example is vitamin C. Humans cannot make vitamin C; we must get it in our diet. The diets of native people contained high amounts of antioxidants, since they ate very little processed foods. Most of the foods they ate came directly from nature. The modern Western diet is very high in processed foods. These foods are very low in antioxidants, and over the years, we have developed an antioxidant deficiency. When this antioxidant deficiency is combined with increased oxidative damage, either through cigarettes, alcohol, stress, or normal aging, it creates a dangerous situation where the free radicals are allowed to damage our DNA, causing breaks and/or mutations, which if not repaired eventually can lead to a breast tumor. This is why every study shows that women who eat more fruits and vegetables have a lower risk of breast cancer! Every study I have ever read shows that anyone who eats more fruits and vegetables has a generalized lower risk of all cancers. As we will show with the beta-carotene/lutein study in the *American Journal of Epidemiology*, those women in the highest 25 percent of these two nutrients slashed their breast cancer risk in *half*!

Three particularly powerful antioxidants are lycopene, lutein, and carotenoids. A study in the *American Journal of Epidemiology* showed that women who had the lowest 25 percent of levels for beta-carotene, lutein, and other carotenoids had double the risk of breast cancer as compared with women who were in the highest 25 percent.[1] *Double the risk!* Beta-carotene is an antioxidant that is in orange-yellow vegetables. This includes carrots, squash, and yams. Lutein is an antioxidant in green leafy vegetables, especially spinach. A Swedish study demonstrated that lutein reduced breast cancer risk in premenopausal women, and lycopene (the red in tomatoes and watermelon) reduced breast cancer risk in postmenopausal women.[2] These fascinating studies demonstrate that the antioxidants in certain fruits and vegetables may reduce your risk of breast cancer by 50 percent.

THE MAGICAL POWER OF TEA

Tea is one of the most popular drinks in the world. Many positive attributes have been given to tea, particularly green tea. The studies we will review show that tea has anticancer effects in animals. The main cancer-fighting ingredient of green tea is EGCG (epi-gallocatechin-3-gallate). The main cancer-fighting ingredients in black tea are polyphenols named *theoflavins*. Animal studies have shown that the EGCG in green tea exerts its anticancer effect by blocking cell reproduction in one of the earliest stages in cancer development. You may recall that in the last step, we discussed how curcumin blocks cancer cell reproduction in another phase of early development. *The exciting finding was that the two of these together were much stronger than either one separately.* In fact, researchers found that when you added both of these nutrients together, you could reduce the amount severalfold and still get significant cancer-killing effects.[3] This means that if you combine the EGCG from green tea with curcumin, your cancer-killing effect is greatly multiplied, since you are inhibiting cancer reproduction at two spots rather than one.

Another interesting fact is that caffeine appears to be a vital ingredient in tea for promotion of cancer-preventing effects.[4] The exact mechanism of why caffeine is important to the cancer-preventing effects of tea is still unknown. It appears that it is best not to get your tea decaffeinated, and perhaps drinking caffeinated green tea is better than a green tea supplement, which usually doesn't contain caffeine. There are trade-offs, however, since a green tea supplement will contain much more EGCG than a cup of green tea.

These two natural ingredients, EGCG (which is in green tea) and curcumin (which is in the spice turmeric), work in conjunction to reduce the risk of cancer through their action of slowing cellular reproduction. Both of these nutrients have very low possibility of side effects. Green tea contains caffeine, but in low amounts, generally one-third to one-fourth as much as in a cup of coffee. And it rarely causes the side effects associated with caffeine, such as the rapid beating of the heart (tachycardia), nervousness, and heart arrhythmias. The side effects from curcumin are very limited and are listed back in Step 10.

Caution: If you have high blood pressure or cardiac disease, then regular green tea is not for you. However, you can still consider a decaffeinated EGCG supplement, which would provide some measure of cancer prevention.

EGCG and curcumin can serve as major pieces to your cancer prevention puzzle. When we combine these nutrients along with the cancer-preventing antioxidants and nutrients that we have discussed in other steps, it forms a valuable plan that could reduce your risk of breast cancer by 90 percent or more. To get the best results, it is important to recognize that these nutrients work together as a team. Therefore, building them into your diet where appropriate is always the first step. The addition of supplements may be a second step for those who wish more aggressive cancer prevention strategies.

THE BOTTOM LINE

Find easy, delicious ways to eat more fruits and vegetables! Here are some simple suggestions:

- Blueberry and/or cherry pie (low sugar added)
- Carrots, broccoli, and cauliflower with dip
- Baked winter squash
- Great salads with fruits, nuts, and mixed greens
- Coleslaw
- Plums, apples, and peaches as snacks
- Sautéed summer squash
- Tomato soup or sauce
- Peppers, broccoli, and asparagus in omelets or quiche
- Strawberries with whipped cream (Remember, I said to have fun. A small amount of whipped cream with a bowl of fresh strawberries is a wonderful dessert.)
- Spinach pie
- Melon and cantaloupe in the morning
- Herbs: basil, oregano, rosemary, parsley, cilantro in any dish possible
- Pumpkin pie (low sugar added)
- Cool watermelon slices on a hot summer day
- Grape juice (or red wine in moderation)
- Vegetable and/or fruit juice

And drink more green tea!

These are just a few ideas to show you how much fun eating antioxidants can really be. Look for ways to add fruits and vegetables to all of your meals.

Increasing your antioxidant intake can be delicious and easy and require little work. Find a grocery or health store that carries organic fruits and vegetables (so you can avoid pesticides and herbicides) and good-quality green teas. This is an integral part of your plan to reduce your risk of breast cancer up to 90 percent.

Avoid Chemicals That Cause Breast Cancer

Since the mid-twentieth century, we have been exposed to thousands of synthetic chemicals. We use these chemicals in plastics, pesticides, weed killers, solvents, and paints, to name just a few uses. Many of these chemicals resemble or act like estrogen, because these chemicals, which are called *xenoestrogens*, are stored in breast tissue and bind to the estrogen receptors in your breasts. Many of these chemicals irreversibly bind to your estrogen receptors and stimulate abnormal cellular reproduction. As we have discussed in previous steps, abnormal cellular reproduction, if allowed to continue, can eventually cause a tumor. We are usually exposed to these chemicals in small doses, but over time they are stored up in our body fat, so over a number of years we can build up significant levels. Since your breasts are 80 percent fat, they are affected more severely than other body organs that contain less fat.

This is how rats are actually given breast cancer in the laboratory. We give them a chemical like dioxin, and we can virtually guarantee that the animals will develop breast cancer. It is not a question of *if* they will develop the disease; it is simply a question of *what* dose of dioxin will cause their breast cells to become abnormal. We are not talking about high-dose exposure, but parts per million and in some cases parts per billion. We know in the laboratory that dioxin causes breast cancer in rats. But no one knows what a safe level of dioxin exposure is for you!

An even greater concern is what happens when you have exposure to several known carcinogens simultaneously. The government does not require industry to study the effects of several chemical carcinogens working in unison. Most toxicology studies are conducted using one carcinogen on a lab animal at a time. However, independent laboratory studies suggest that these carcinogenic chemicals have a synergistic effect. That means that with exposure to several chemicals, it takes less of each to cause cancer than if you had a single exposure to a single chemical. If you're thinking that you haven't been exposed to these chemicals because you don't work in a factory or industrial setting, you're kidding yourself. We have all been exposed to numerous carcinogens and continue to be exposed every day. It is simply a matter of how much!

Studies have shown that dioxin, DDE, and PCB (very dangerous chemicals) have been detected in ice cream, fried chicken, pizza, and hamburgers.[1] This study shows that these chemicals are spread throughout our food supply. That's because they are everywhere in our environment. Unless you have been locked away in a monastery in Tibet, you have these chemicals in your breasts. Let's review which chemicals are the most dangerous, how to avoid those chemicals, and steps you can take to block these carcinogens from harming your breasts.

WHAT CHEMICALS ARE DANGEROUS?

Unfortunately, there are so many dangerous chemicals in our environment that we could devote a whole book to discussing the chemicals we are exposed to and their dangers. What we will do in this step is give you a primer, so to speak, on the major groups of chemicals that can harm your breasts and how to avoid them.

Dioxin and Dioxin-Like PCBs

Dioxin is a chemical made from chlorine.[2] Dioxin is used to make plastic wrap, pesticides, wood preservatives, bleached paper, and a host of other industrial products. Through these industrial uses, dioxin is released into our streams and lakes. It is concentrated in the meat, dairy, and fish we eat. In addition, by burning plastic, we release dioxins into the air, where it may further contaminate soil, water, and eventually us. Perhaps the most tragic industrial exposure happened in my home state of Michigan in the 1970s. PCBs (polychlorinated biphenyls) were mistakenly placed in cattle feed. The cattle were fed this feed, and we then consumed the milk from the cattle. Since that time, studies have consistently shown that the majority of women in Michigan have elevated PCBs in their breast milk. Industrial accidents like this are tragic but (as far as we know) fairly rare.

A more common problem is that we are exposed to trace amounts of dioxin and dioxin-like chemicals every day through our food.[3] Even more disturbing is that a study has found that "exposure of an average 6-year-old was especially high due to a child's lower body weight."[4] It's worth noting that chemical exposure often produces symptoms in children and pets first. Because they are lower in body weight, they do not tolerate as high of an exposure as an adult. One of the subtle questions I always ask my patients is if their children or pets have been sick. Many times after the house has been sprayed with a pesticide, the dog or cat will develop leukemia and/or lymphoma. This is a sign that the adults and children have had significant exposure as well.

A Canadian study of 400 women found a "clear association with the amount of PCBs measured in breast tissue and breast cancer risk."[5] Along with dioxin and PCBs, there are several other chemicals that occur in plastics that may be carcinogenic. These include chemicals used in plastic milk jugs, bottles, plastic can linings, plastic wrap, and deli wrap.

Pesticides: DDT and DDE

DDT and DDE have been banned for use in the United States because of their known reproductive toxicity. Yet we allow them to be manufactured in the United States and shipped to foreign countries, especially Latin America, where they are sprayed on fruit and vegetables and then imported back to the United States. A sad, but true, state of affairs.

Many pesticides have estrogen-like effects. Organochlorines have been shown to cause breast cancer in lab animals. (DDT is a "banned" organochlorine.) A fascinating study was done on seals that ate herring contaminated with dioxin-like organochlorines in the Baltic. This two-year study showed that the seals' natural killer cell function was reduced 20 to 50 percent.[6] Natural killer cells are responsible for detecting and destroying early cancers. When you reduce natural killer cell function by 20 to 50 percent, you are significantly impairing your immune system's response to cancer. This increases the likelihood that a cancer will escape detection and/or destruction and eventually become a tumor. A study published in the *Journal of the National Cancer Institute*

Table 13.1 Organochlorine Pesticides

Aldrin	Endrin
Chlordane	Hexachlorobenzene
DDT and DDE	Heptachlor
Dieldrin	Lindane
Endosulfan I and II	Mirex

Source: W. J. Rea, *Chemical Sensitivity,* Volume 4
(Boca Raton, FL: Lewis Publishers, 1996), 2016.

showed that breast cancer was *400 percent* higher in the women with the highest levels of the organochlorine DDE in their breast tissue.[7] Researchers have found that organochlorines improves the enzyme that converts estrogen to the 4 OH and 16 OH metabolites. We have already seen that the 4 OH metabolite appears to be a carcinogen. We have also seen that an increase in the 16 OH levels increases your risk of breast cancer by reducing your estrogen metabolite index (EMI). For a list of organochlorine pesticides, see Table 13.1.

ESTROGENS IN OUR MEAT AND MILK

Farmers routinely give estrogen to cattle to make them gain weight more quickly or to help them produce more milk. Since the farmer gets paid by the pound, not the quality, the object is to get cattle fat as quickly as possible. Dairy farmers also get paid for their milk by the pound, so the more milk the cow produces, the more money the dairy farmer makes. Unfortunately, these hormones go into the meat and milk that you and your family consume every day. Once inside of you, guess where these estrogens go? Some of them go to your breasts and attach to your estrogen receptors. This stimulation causes increased cell reproduction. The more meat and milk you consume, the stronger the estrogenic stimulation. Who drinks the most milk? Our children! Some scientists have speculated that this is one reason why women are attaining menarche (the first menstruation) at younger and younger ages. They are getting supplemental estrogen in their food, and we just haven't recognized it.

WHAT CAN WE DO?

Given the dangers presented by these chemicals and the difficulty in avoiding them, what in the world should a reasonable person do? In my opinion, the evidence is clear. You should reduce or avoid these chemicals in any way possible! Let's review some simple steps you can take to reduce your chemical exposure and protect yourself and your family.

- *Eat organic fruits and vegetables.* Organic fruits and vegetables have not been sprayed with pesticides or herbicides. This means that they are free of organochlorines and related compounds. These vegetables and fruits are more expensive, but worth every penny. To reduce your costs, you can join an organic food co-op so that you can buy in bulk. If you don't want to join a co-op, then find the closest health food store or supermarket that has organic produce and purchase your fruits and vegetables there. Not only will your fruits and vegetables be free from pesticides and

herbicides, but studies have shown that organic produce
is actually higher in vitamins and minerals than
nonorganic produce.[8] Organic milk is also available
at health food stores and in an increasing number of
traditional supermarkets.

- *Eat "clean" meat and poultry.* Organic meat and poultry
can be very expensive to buy. I recommend that you buy
"clean" meat. What do I mean by clean? Clean meat and
poultry have been raised without estrogen supplementation and with a minimum of chemical exposure. They
have not routinely been given *antibiotics*. By definition,
these products are not organic, since organic meat and
poultry must be fed organic feed. Clean meat and poultry isn't perfect, but it's a darn sight better and safer
than commercial meat and poultry.

What I do is buy my meat and poultry directly from farmers I
have actually interviewed so that I know how and what they feed their
animals. In this way, I am reasonably certain of reducing the amount
of pesticides, estrogens, and antibiotics I consume in the meat and
poultry I eat. I get safer, better-tasting meat and poultry at a lower
cost than in the supermarket. This is a win-win situation. It takes a
little more work in the beginning, but is well worth it. A good place
to start for either clean or organic meat is your local farmer's mar-
ket. You can interview the local farmers directly and discuss with
them how they raise their livestock. You might also want to contact
your local organic food club, since they may know local sources of
clean and/or reasonably priced organic meat and poultry.

- *Do not spray pesticides or herbicides around your house,
lawn, or garden.* Think before you act! If you have bugs in

your house or garden, you do not have to live with them.
There are plenty of safe, natural, organic ways to get rid of
the bugs and/or weeds without getting rid of you or your
children. If you needed further proof, studies show that
children who live in households where the lawn and garden are routinely sprayed have a *600 percent higher* risk of
childhood leukemia than children who live in houses that
do not routinely spray. Get rid of the bugs and weeds
organically and keep your children and yourself safe.

· *Avoid plastic wrap whenever possible.* I know it isn't easy,
but try to avoid plastic wrap and plastic bottles where
possible. Does anyone remember the milk carton? Instead
of using plastic wrap, use other types of containers. Never
microwave anything in plastic wrap or in a plastic bowl.
Use the appropriate microwave-safe glass. Do not store
water in plastic jugs or bottles; use glass bottles.

· *Block the toxic effects of dioxin.* I3C and DIM have been
shown to block the effects of dioxin in breast tissue.[9]
Dioxin and dioxin-like chemicals attach to the "Ah"
receptor on breast cells. We discussed the "Ah" receptor
in Step 5 in great detail and the fact that when activated,
the "Ah" receptor promotes breast cell growth. Dioxin
binds to the "Ah" receptor, causing abnormal instruc-
tions to go to your DNA and causing your breast cells to
reproduce wildly and eventually create a tumor. We
know from studies that if I3C and DIM are present in
the body, they can block the majority of dioxin's harmful
effects on breast tissue. As we reviewed in Step 5, the way
I3C and DIM does this is by binding to the "Ah" receptor
and thereby preventing dioxin from attaching.[10] The only
problem is that I3C and DIM do not bind the "Ah"

receptor for long periods of time (unlike dioxin, which may bind irreversibly). Taking moderate amounts of vegetables and/or supplements containing I3C and/or DIM over a long period of time is more protective than taking a large dose over a shorter period. (For example, eating 3 pounds of broccoli today and then not eating it again for a year will not get the desired result. It is better for you to eat several servings of cruciferous vegetables per week, every week, as a part of your everyday diet.) We have reviewed the controversy regarding supplemental I3C versus DIM. The scientific studies, however, are fairly clear on the fact that DIM protects the "Ah" receptor as well as supplemental I3C. (See Step 5 concerning dose and precautions of supplemental DIM/I3C.)

THE BOTTOM LINE

In my opinion, the research is clear concerning dioxin, organochlorines, PCBs, and dioxin-like chemicals: *these chemicals may cause breast cancer!* Since we do not know what dose is safe, or indeed if any dose is safe, and suspect that these chemicals act in a synergistic manner, *avoidance* is the first and best treatment. You can reduce exposure to these chemicals by following this advice:

- Eat organic fruits and vegetables.
- Use organic pest and weed solutions.
- Drink organic milk and milk products.
- Find clean meat and poultry produced by someone you can interview and trust.

- Think before you use any solvent, cleaner, spray, degreaser, or paint in your house or your life. Read all labels carefully. Use natural and organic alternatives that are available at larger health stores.
- Eat cruciferous vegetables every day or several times a week. (Avoid cruciferous vegetables if you are pregnant or breast-feeding.)
- Consider DIM supplementation if you cannot or will not eat cruciferous vegetables on a regular basis (see Step 5).

This information is meant as an eye-opener, not as an exhaustive review of the dangers presented by xenoestrogen chemicals. You alone are responsible for the health of you and your family. You must know what you are eating, how it is grown, and where it came from. You should know what chemicals are used and/or sprayed around your house, garden, and lawn, as they can pose a significant cancer risk to your family. Do not take the manufacturer's word on this. Pest control companies and lawn companies will rarely be up front on the possible dangers involved. *Buyer beware!*

In short, you can, with very little work, avoid many exposures to these chemicals and improve the quality of your life in the process. Unfortunately, all of us will continue to be exposed to dioxin and other organochlorines every time we eat out. You can help block the harmful effects of these exposures by eating cruciferous vegetables several times a week and/or taking an I3C or DIM supplement. Include in your daily diet as many organic fruits and vegetables as possible, since the antioxidants in these foods will help reduce your risk of breast cancer.

Avoidance of chemicals is another dramatic step you can take to reduce your risk of breast cancer by 90 percent or more.

Raise Your B_{12} and Folate Levels

A study published in *Cancer, Epidemiology, Biomarkers, and Prevention* showed that low levels of vitamin B_{12} appear to be a risk factor for breast cancer. That study found that there was an increased risk of breast cancer in the 20 percent of postmenopausal women who had the lowest B_{12} levels as compared with women with higher levels.[1] B_{12} and folate deficiency could increase your risk for breast cancer in three ways:

1. Low B_{12} may contribute to low thymidine levels in the body. Thymidine is important in making and repairing genes. We need a special type of folate (also called folic acid) to make thymidine, and we need B_{12} to make this special type of folate. If you are low in B_{12}, your thymidine may run low. If your body runs low in thymidine, you can't repair your genes correctly. This may cause a strand of gene to break, causing a mutation in that gene. We have already talked about how breast cancer starts with genetic damage and mutation. Therefore, the more poorly you repair these breaks, the greater the risk of a genetic mutation in your breast cells that could be the start of a cancer.

2. Your tumor suppressor genes must have methyl groups in order to function. Two substances that are very important donors of methyl are B$_{12}$ and folate. Methyl groups, it should be noted, are essential to various processes in the body. In this case, B$_{12}$ and folate contribute methyl groups to your tumor suppressor genes, improving their function so that they are more active [up regulated] not sluggish [down regulated]. Studies have shown that the DNA found in the tissue of breast cancer has a significantly lower number of these methyl groups compared with normal breast tissue.[2]

3. Studies have shown that increasing the methyl groups on tumor promoter genes turns down their function.[3] So, not only does the methyl created by B$_{12}$ and folate improve tumor *suppressor* genes, but it also may reduce the action of tumor *promoter* genes. You want your tumor suppressor genes to be turned up and your tumor promoter genes to be turned down. These studies suggest that B$_{12}$ and folate do just that!

An interesting study was done as part of the Iowa Women's Health Study. This study concluded that as long as women who drank alcohol had enough folate, they were not at an increased risk of breast cancer. It showed that women who drank 4 grams of alcohol a day but had the highest folate levels were at no greater risk of breast cancer than a woman who did not drink. However, women who drank only 2 grams of alcohol per day but were in the lowest 25 percent of folate consumption had nearly a *60 percent higher risk* of breast cancer.[4] We know that the detoxification of alcohol depletes folate. Therefore, the more alcohol you drink, the more folate you need. It is unfortunate that the vast majority of American women are low in folate. That is why it is now recommended that pregnant women take at least 400 micrograms of folate daily. Folate has been shown to reduce neurological defects in newborns. The media have done a fairly good job letting women know that if they are pregnant they need extra folic acid; what they don't know (and you now do know) is that any woman can benefit from extra folic acid, especially if she drinks alcohol.

HOW DO YOU KNOW IF YOU ARE LOW IN B_{12} AND FOLATE?

To find out your B_{12} and folate levels, you need to have your levels measured. If you go to your family doctor and ask for B_{12} and folate levels, he or she will do a blood test for B_{12} and folate levels. If your levels are low or low normal, it is obvious that you need B_{12} and folate supplementation. But if they are "within normal range," that does not necessarily mean you have enough B_{12} and folate. The reason for this is that serum B_{12} and folate levels have such a wide range of normal. You can be within "normal range" and still not have enough folate and B_{12} to turn up your tumor suppressor genes and turn down your tumor promoter genes. To fully evaluate your B_{12} and folate levels, your doctor should do tests that measure your homocystine, methylmalonate, and tetrahydrofolate levels. These levels more accurately reflect your true B_{12}/folate status. Elevated homocystine is a risk factor for heart disease and cancer, since it indicates that you are functionally low in B_{12} and folate. Elevated methylmalonate levels suggest a functional B_{12} deficiency, since B_{12} is required for the conversion of methylmalonate. Tetrahydrofolate is the type of folate that is active in the body. Millions of Americans have trouble converting folate to tetrahydrofolate. If your tetrahydrofolate levels are low, you may require a tetrahydrofolate supplement or much higher doses of folic acid.

WHAT CAN YOU DO IF YOUR B$_{12}$ AND FOLATE LEVELS ARE LOW?

Upping Your Levels Through Diet

Dietary sources of folate are green leafy vegetables, peas, beans, and enriched cereals. Sources of B$_{12}$ are meats, including liver and beef, fish, and fortified cereals. To give you an idea of how much you need, 3 ounces of liver contains 60 micrograms of B$_{12}$, 3 ounces of beef contains 2.1 micrograms of B$_{12}$, and 3 ounces of salmon or trout contains approximately 5 micrograms of B$_{12}$. Though liver is extremely high in B$_{12}$, the truth of the matter is that unless the liver is from an organic cow, it is probably not worth eating.

What About Supplements?

Since most American women are deficient in both B$_{12}$ and folate, supplementation of both makes sense. B$_{12}$ and folate are very easily and inexpensively supplemented. There are essentially no known side effects to reasonable doses of either. Because folate deficiency is widespread throughout the American population, supplementation with 400 micrograms to 1 milligram per day makes sense. B_{12} can be supplemented at approximately 1,000 micrograms daily sublingual (under the tongue). My preferred type of B_{12} supplement is methylcobalamin. The more common form of B_{12} supplement is cyanocobalamin, which is B_{12} combined with small amounts of cyanide. While these small amounts of cyanide have never been shown to have any deleterious effects, it makes sense to me to use the methylcobalamin form, since we are trying to increase the amounts of methyl groups available within the body. If you use alcohol in moderation, it makes sense to supplement B_{12} and folate. The dose I use in the office is 400 micrograms to 1 mlligram daily. For my patients that drink alcohol frequently, I often recommend a higher dose of folate (1 to 3 milligrams daily) and B_{12} (1,000 to 3,000 micrograms daily). As we have discussed, those women who drank alcohol and were in the lowest 20 percent of folate intake had a *60 percent higher* risk of breast cancer.

The moral of this story is do not allow B_{12} and folate deficiency to increase your risk of breast cancer! Folate and B_{12} supplementation is cheap and easy, and if done in moderation, it has very low potential for side effects. There is really no reason why you should allow B_{12} and folate deficiency to increase your risk of breast cancer.

Now let's move on to see how improving the "ninjas" of your immune system may help reduce your breast cancer risk by 90 percent or more.

Strengthen Your Cancer-Fighting Immune Cells

The most important step you can take to improve your immunity is to improve your natural killer cell function—what doctors call your *NK function*.

WHAT ARE NATURAL KILLER CELLS?

Natural killer (NK) cells are the "special forces" of the immune system. Like military special forces, they are small in numbers but very important in the "seek and destroy" mission of the immune system. NK cells are responsible for recognizing intruders, attacking those intruders, and destroying them. When NK cells attack, they produce chemicals that stimulate the remainder of your immune system to move to the area of the body that is infected. This is important for defense from viruses, bacteria, parasites, and cancer. NK cells are responsible for detecting the 200 cancers each of us develop every day. Of the trillions of cells in our body, millions become sick, damaged, or mutated daily. The majority of these sick cells self-destruct in a process we call apoptosis. Cancer cells lose this ability to self-destruct and just keep multiplying.

Therefore, several hundred cancers may begin each and every day. It is the job of NK cells to recognize these deformed, mutated cells (cancer cells) and destroy them.

There are two important factors in determining NK cell effectiveness: the number of NK cells and the function of those cells. Like the military special forces, you can have two problems: (1) not enough soldiers or (2) enough soldiers, but soldiers that do not fight very well.

Of these two problems, the most dangerous is soldiers that do not fight well—in other words, you have enough NK cells, but they don't function well. AIDS research has shown that a person can be surprisingly healthy with very few NK cells as long as normal NK function is maintained. If a person with AIDS loses NK cell function, even if NK numbers are near or above normal, that person can develop cancers such as sarcoma and die. In this step, we will focus on how to improve your NK cell function so that your body can easily detect and kill off breast cancer *before* these cancers endanger your life.

DO YOU KNOW YOUR
NATURAL KILLER CELL FUNCTION LEVEL?

Anyone can have their NK cell function measured. A blood sample is simply taken, and the NK cells that are removed (within 24 hours) are subjected to stimuli to see how well they attack. In the right laboratory this is easily done, even though the NK cell function test is not a routine test and is one that most doctors and/or laboratories may not be familiar with. Measurement of your NK cell function is actually fairly easy as long as you have a doctor and laboratory familiar with the procedure.

WHAT LOWERS NATURAL KILLER CELL FUNCTION?

No one is absolutely sure of all the factors that reduce NK cell function. We can point to some of the usual suspects: stress, poor diet, nutritional deficiency, lack of sleep, viral infection, and depression. Significant research has been done on NK cell function in AIDS, but very little research has been done on the factors that depress NK cells in a less sick population.

HOW CAN YOU IMPROVE YOUR NATURAL KILLER CELL FUNCTION?

Research has shown several supplements that improve NK cell function. Before we discuss these, let's make sure that you have covered some of the basics.

- Increase your sleep. (See our discussion of melatonin in Step 11.)
- Reduce stress.
- Improve your diet based on the information in this book.
- Reduce or regulate depression by keeping your blood sugar stable and by using nutrients to maintain normal brain chemistry.

WHAT ABOUT SUPPLEMENTS?

Glutathione (GTH)

GTH is a three-amino-acid antioxidant that is vital for detoxification and cellular protection. Studies have shown that glutathione improves natural killer cell function.

How Do You Know If You Are Low in Glutathione? There are several laboratory studies available that measure glutathione levels. If you are over 40 and have been on the Standard America Diet (SAD), odds are you are deficient in this important nutrient. This deficiency is compounded by alcohol use (the liver requires GTH to detoxify alcohol), toxins, smoking, and medications. GTH is a very important antioxidant in the detoxification of estrogen. Remember, all estrogen is detoxified in the liver to its metabolites. If you are low in GTH, your detoxification slows down.

How Can You Improve Your GTH Levels?

- *NAC (N-acetylcysteine).* This is an amino acid that is important in the production of glutathione and is well absorbed when given orally. The usual dose is 500 milligrams once or twice daily. Side effects are very rare but can include indigestion.
- *Glutamine.* This is another amino acid that is important for glutathione production within the body. The usual dose is 500 milligrams once or twice daily. Side effects

can include irritability and sleep disturbances. Therefore, avoid use in the evening and discontinue if you
become nervous or irritable.

- GTH. Glutathione does come as a supplement, but is
  more poorly absorbed than NAC. If you use GTH as a
  supplement, make sure it is in *reduced* form, since only
  reduced glutathione functions as an antioxidant.
  Caution: Diabetics should not take GTH supplements
  without the expressed consent of their physicians, since
  GTH may alter their blood sugar. The usual dose of
  GTH is 75 to 100 milligrams once or twice daily. Side
  effects are rare, but GTH can affect blood sugar levels
  (see above) and may increase detoxification. Never start
  on high levels of GTH, as we want the body to detoxify
  slowly. (Rapid detoxification may increase fatigue, cause
  muscle pain, and cloud thinking.)

- *Lipoic acid.* This is an antioxidant that helps recharge
  glutathione into the reduced form. When glutathione
  soaks up a free radical, it is oxidized. Lipoic acid absorbs
  the free radical from glutathione, converting it back to
  the reduced form—the form that can function as an
  antioxidant. The usual dose is 100 milligrams one to
  three times daily. Side effects are rare but can include
  indigestion and stomach upset.

I cannot stress enough that quality supplements make all the
difference in the world. There are "tricks" that some manufacturers use to reduce the price of supplements. But if you buy glutathione that is not in reduced form, you are wasting your money!

IP-6 (Inositol hexaphosphate)

IP-6 is the nutrient that results when six phosphate groups are attached to the B vitamin inositol. IP-6 helps prevent breast cancer by controlling the rate of cellular division. Studies have shown IP-6 effective in inhibiting both estrogen receptor positive and estrogen receptor negative breast cell lines. IP-6 also improves natural killer cell function. Studies have shown that IP-6 improves the function of your natural killer cells. Cereals and legumes are the richest natural sources of IP-6. Taken in supplement form, the usual dose of IP-6 is two capsules twice daily. Few side effects have been observed with IP-6, since it is simply a B vitamin attached to six groups of phosphate. However, you should not use IP-6 if you have an autoimmune disorder or if you are pregnant or breast-feeding.[1]

Clinically I have used IP-6 on hundreds of patients who were found to have low NK cell function. Combining natural therapies to correct nutritional deficiencies in conjunction with IP-6 has allowed many of those patients to regain more normal NK cell function. Improved NK cell function enables them to fight off infection and cancer.

MGN-3

MGN-3 is a nutrient that is originally derived from a combination of a rice bran extract with an extract made from shitake mushrooms. Studies have shown that 3,000 milligrams of MGN-3 per day increased the activity of NK cells by as much as 300 percent.[2] MGN-3 is a synthetic supplement; therefore, it is not directly available from food. The usual dose is 1,000 milligrams per day in divided doses for the first 2 weeks, then 1,000 milligrams per day thereafter. No toxic side effects have been noted in studies done with MGN-3. It would be prudent to avoid MGN-3 if you have an autoimmune disease or if you are allergic to mushrooms. Remember to use all the nutrients we discussed above under the supervision of a health care provider who understands nutritional therapy.

THE BOTTOM LINE

I recommend that you know what your natural killer cell function level is. If it is low, take the following steps to improve it:

- Increase and improve your sleep.
- Reduce stress.
- Improve your diet.
- Resolve depression.
- If after 3 to 6 months, your NK cell function has not improved upon recheck, then consider the addition of supplements, including glutathione, lipoic acid, IP-6, and/or MGN-3.

By improving your NK cell function, you increase the likelihood that your body's immune system will detect and destroy early breast cancers. Most doctors do not directly work with natural killer cell function; therefore, they will not be familiar with the research or how to measure NK cell function. Make sure this test is done by a doctor and laboratory that knows what an NK cell function test is and what it's used for. Prior to implementing any supplement program, make sure you consult a physician who understands nutritional therapy and can give recommendations based on your specific needs.

Detoxify to Reduce Your Breast Cancer Risk

We have already discussed that estrogen is detoxified in the liver to its metabolites via the P450 pathway. It is along this P450 pathway that estrogen is metabolized as either 2 OH, 4 OH, or 16 OH. Significant amounts of these estrogen metabolites then go back into your bloodstream. To maintain balance, your body must be able to get rid of excessive estrogen and estrogen metabolites. It does this through a detoxification pathway named the glucuronidation pathway. Once estrogen is detoxified via the glucuronidation pathway, it is excreted in the stool and urine. If you are unable to get rid of these metabolites, they are reabsorbed from the bowel and reenter your circulation. Millions of women have the complaint of chronic constipation. Many women have a movement every two to five days and think that it is "normal." Yet, the longer you allow these estrogen metabolites to stay in the body, the more they will be reabsorbed and reenter circulation. This, of course, increases the levels of estrogen metabolites in your blood. We have already discussed that the lower your levels of the "bad" 16 OH and 4 OH metabolites, the better. Once these metabolites are excreted into your bowel, the key is to eliminate them so they are not reabsorbed.

CONSTIPATION AND THE "SICK BOWEL"

It is hard for many women to realize how constipation can be so damaging to their health and how your bowel can possibly affect your breasts. The ancient Chinese put it bluntly when they said, "Death begins in the bowel." Millions of American women have chronic constipation because their bowel is "sick." If your bowel is sick, you cannot absorb the nutrients necessary for health, your immunity suffers, and your energy plummets. A sick bowel has an overgrowth of "bad bacteria." These "bad bacteria" produce an enzyme named *beta-glucuronidase*. Normal substances like hormones and harmful chemicals like pesticides normally bind to glucarate in the liver and are removed via our stool. If the harmful enzyme beta-glucuronidase is high, toxins and hormones cannot bind to glucarate and are kept in our body. This increases both the levels of free estrogen and the levels of estrogen metabolites, not to mention other toxins that remain in our body. Elevated levels of free estrogen and/or beta-glucuronidase are associated with an increased risk of breast cancer.[1] A sick bowel also loses its peristalsis, the normal muscular contraction of the bowel that keeps waste products moving. A reduction of peristalsis also causes hormones and toxins to stay in the bowel for longer periods of time. As we discussed before, many of them get reabsorbed.

Why Do Millions of Women Have a "Sick Bowel"?

There are many ways your bowel can become "sick." The most common reason in Western societies is overuse of antibiotics. Baby boomers and every generation since have grown up with antibiotics both as prescriptions and in our food. Most of us have had many courses of prescription antibiotics by the time we are adults. Those of you with allergies or chronic ear/throat problems had multiple courses of antibiotics during your childhood. Some of you, as teens, had years of antibiotics for acne. Then with sexual activity you had urinary tract infections and vaginal infections, all requiring even more antibiotics. What you have not been told is that every time you take an antibiotic, it not only kills the "bad" bacteria that we are trying to kill, but also kills the "good" bacteria that are vital for digestion. This is especially evident in women: you know that the first thing that happens when you take an antibiotic is you get a vaginal yeast infection. The reason for this is that the antibiotic kills off the "good" bacteria that helps protect your vagina, but does not kill yeast. This allows the yeast to overgrow and causes an infection.

Likewise, after many courses of antibiotics, the good bacteria in your bowel becomes decimated. Because your bowel depends on good bacteria for normal function, it starts to become "sick" once the good bacteria start to get killed off. As the good bacteria are killed, bad bacteria or yeast, which are resistant to antibiotics, overgrow, thereby reducing the absorption of nutrients from your food and producing toxins, which cause a number of adverse health affects. Good bacteria produce nutrients that are necessary to feed the inner lining of your digestive tract. (This is one of the few places in the body where nutrients are not received directly from the blood.) As the good bacteria become decimated, they produce fewer nutrients. As the nutrient levels drop, your bowel cannot get the proper nourishment and starts to become more damaged, leading to the point where function becomes seriously impaired.

Doctors have been ignorant of this problem; therefore, they have never told you to replace the good bacteria to maintain proper bowel health. Good bacteria can be easily replaced by eating foods that are high in good bacteria, like yogurt, buttermilk, or kefir, or by taking probiotics (good-bacteria supplements). There are literally dozens of studies that show that postantibiotic super infections are dramatically reduced with probiotic supplementation. Many of you have had a sick bowel for years, possibly decades. If your bowel is sick, it is impossible to be healthy. If you do not actively repair the damage that has been done to your bowel, you will be sick for the rest of your life. Repairing a sick bowel is not always easy, but you can start by eating some organic yogurt every day or taking a live probiotic supplement. Some of you will need to have treatment for the overgrowth of yeast or pathogenic bad bacteria along with supplementation of good bacteria.

As many as 90 million Americans complain of bowel problems, with approximately 45 million having irritable bowel syndrome (IBS). (Symptoms of IBS are bloating, gas, diarrhea, and abdominal pain.) Millions of you have been told by your doctor that IBS is in your head, but it results, in many cases, from destruction of good bacteria and the overgrowth of bad bacteria and/or yeast.

There are other contributing factors to a "sick bowel":

- *Lack of fiber.* The Standard American Diet (SAD) contains less fiber than any diet in human history. We need fiber to make our bowel function properly.
- *Insufficient intake of water.* Many of you drink caffeinated drinks like coffee or soda, which further dehy-

drate. Proper amounts of water are necessary for normal digestion and bowel function.

• *Too little exercise.* Americans get less exercise than any civilization in human history. Exercise is vital for stimulating the bowel and contributing to normal movements.

• *Thyroid problems.* Millions of you have subtle low thyroid (hypothyroid). You are cold all the time. You gain weight easily. You are chronically constipated. Many of you have had blood tests that said you were "normal." A new study in the *British Medical Journal* suggests that our definition of "normal" is incorrect. Your thyroid-stimulating hormone (TSH), the hormone produced in your brain that tells your thyroid that you need more thyroid hormone, has been considered normal if the levels measured between 0.4 and 5.5. A new study suggests that "normal" TSH should be between 1 and 2, not 5.5. This means that many of you have been told your thyroid is normal when in fact you have mild hypothyroidism. If you are cold all the time, gain weight easily, and have dry skin and chronic constipation, have your thyroid levels rechecked. If your TSH is above 2, consider low-dose thyroid supplementation. An even better test is a 24-hour urine evaluation of thyroid function. This detects subtle low thyroid that blood levels can miss. The evidence is mounting that low thyroid may be a risk factor for breast cancer. This may be why a recent study in the *Journal of Nutrition* has shown that seaweed may reduce breast cancer risk; seaweed contains iodine, which may improve thyroid function if a person is deficient in iodine.

THE BOTTOM LINE

- You cannot be healthy if your bowel is sick.
- Chronic constipation increases the reabsorption of estrogen and estrogen metabolites, thereby increasing your risk of breast cancer.
- The abnormal "bad" bacteria in a sick bowel produces the enzyme beta-glucuronidase, which reduces detoxification of estrogen and *increases* your risk of breast cancer.
- A sick bowel cannot absorb the nutrients and antioxidants necessary for health. Therefore, your immunity drops, which *increases* your risk of breast cancer.
- Millions of you have developed a "sick bowel" through the overuse of antibiotics, which has killed your good bacteria.
- If your bowel is overgrown with yeast and/or "bad bacteria," you must have the correct therapy to reduce the concentration of both types of pathogens.
- Increase your fiber, water, and walking to help improve chronic constipation. If you complain of being cold when others are not, if you gain weight easily, if your skin is dry, and if you have chronic constipation, have your thyroid levels checked.
- As the ancient Chinese said, "Death begins in the bowel." To reduce your risk of breast cancer by 90 percent or more, you must actively work to restore bowel health.

Eat Right to Reduce Risk

At my lectures throughout the country, I have found that most women, deep down, know that increasing fruits and vegetables in their diet will reduce their risk of breast cancer. The sad thing is that even though they know this in their heart, they don't do anything about it. The most common reason they give is that they are "too busy." In this step, we will not only summarize the foods that help you prevent breast cancer, but also give you easy tips to incorporate these foods into your everyday diet. Let's face it, if the diet is too strict or too hard to follow, you won't do it for very long. We will try to make this *simple*! Investment advisors always tell you to put whatever amount of money you can into your retirement account. If you can fully fund it every year, terrific! If you cannot, then at least put whatever you can afford into your retirement account and make it a yearly habit. This is an excellent analogy for changing your diet to prevent breast cancer. My hope is that you can eat five servings a day of fruits and vegetables; but if you cannot or will not, then eat as many servings as you can.

A very large study called the Nurses Health Study found that premenopausal women who ate five or more servings of fruits and vegetables per day had a lower risk of breast cancer than those who ate fewer than two servings.[1] If eating five servings a day significantly lowers your breast cancer risk, why don't you do it?

Women give several reasons. Here are the two most common reasons that we hear.

- *Not enough time.* For some reason, people think that preparing fruits and vegetables takes time. In reality, nothing can be simpler. How difficult is it to prewash some vegetables—for example, broccoli, carrots, and snow peas (you can choose whatever vegetables you like)—and use them as a snack throughout the day with some nice, tasty, low-fat, organic ranch dressing as a dip? It is great tasting and fabulous for your health. We have already discussed how important the cruciferous vegetables are to converting your estrogen to the "good" 2 OH metabolite. Using broccoli and cauliflower as a snack is a great way to increase your cruciferous vegetable intake. Have a peach with breakfast, an apple as a snack, strawberries with cream or a small amount of whipped cream for dessert, or even a piece of low-sugar pumpkin pie. All of these are delicious, easy ways to get more antioxidants in your diet.
- *Vegetables are boring.* Vegetables are only boring if you allow them to be. Have fun with your food and make sure it is delicious. There are many easy recipes available that show you how to make vegetables more interesting. A common misconception is that to be healthy, you must eat your vegetables plain. I will happily show you ways to make them delicious if you promise me to eat more of them. Coleslaw is a great way to increase cabbage in your diet. Yes, I know that coleslaw has a small

amount of sugar. Keep the amount of sugar as low as possible and use a low-fat organic coleslaw dressing. As for salads, you can buy premade gourmet organic salad mixes already prepared at the health store. Use organic tomatoes, broccoli spears, a small amount of fresh fruit (such as tangerine slices), and a few walnuts. Top this off with low-fat organic salad dressing and you have a tremendous food for the prevention of breast cancer. Wasn't that easy? You can make this salad twice a week. Salads will keep for two or three days in an appropriate container in the refrigerator. Instead of having a candy bar, a cigarette, or soda during your work break, have a piece of fruit. It is delicious, high energy, and contains antioxidants, fiber, vitamins, and minerals. Have a piece of fresh fruit daily for breakfast. Slice up a large bowl of fruit and keep it in the refrigerator. Finally, have sliced fruit and/or fruit pie for dessert. Sliced strawberries with cream or a small amount of whipped cream are a wonderful way to end a meal. If you choose to have pumpkin, blueberry, or cherry pie, make sure it is homemade, baked with organic fruit and low sugar. Many commercial pies are basically artificial fruit filling that do not contain antioxidants; they are very high in sugar and are worthless.

We've been brainwashed! Most of us were raised at a time when we were bombarded by billions of dollars of advertising, conditioning us to buy foods that if consumed on a regular basis would kill us. When we were children, we saw thousands of commercials for sugar-coated cereals, fast foods, candy bars, and more. The result of all this conditioning is that we spend money to eat foods that are harmful to our health. (For the record, I want to state that there is nothing wrong with having a burger and fries or a high-sugar dessert occasionally. If done in moderation, these can be a fun "sin.") The problem is that for many of you, these have become staples of your diet. Like alcohol, a small amount now and then can be one of life's little pleasures.

DIETARY RECOMMENDATIONS

Always Use Organic Fruits and Vegetables

In Step 13, we discussed how pesticides help promote breast cancer development, how you cannot wash these pesticides off, and how once consumed, the pesticides stay with you for life. Even worse, most pesticides are stored in fat; therefore, the concentrations in your breasts will be 30 to 1,000 times higher than the concentrations in your blood. One good rule to follow for fruits and vegetables is: Eat organic! In addition to avoiding the pesticides and herbicides, studies have shown organic vegetables and fruits are higher in vitamins and minerals than regular produce. Farming practices have changed dramatically in our lifetime. Farmers now plant the same crop on the same land year after year. They can do this by using chemical fertilizers, which help the crop to grow, but the land becomes depleted in trace minerals and therefore, even though the potato (for example) looks the same as an organic potato, it does not have the nutrient value.

Change Your Oil

No, I am not talking about your car's oil. You are eating too much fat and especially the *wrong* type of fat. Most of the oil in the Standard American Diet (SAD) is omega-6 fatty acids. The omega-6 fatty acids include corn, soy, cottonseed, safflower, and peanut oil. Most baked goods and fried foods in the United States contain these types of oil. Margarine is made from omega-6 fatty acids that have been "tortured." Here's what I mean: Oil does not stay solid at room temperature; it is a liquid. To keep margarine solid at room temperature, manufacturers torture the oil via a process named hydrogenation. Hydrogenated oils are being linked to a host of health problems, including an increased risk of breast cancer. Researchers found that those women who ate the most polyunsaturated fat had a 69 percent increased risk of breast cancer.[2] Originally, these hydrogenated oils were thought to be better for you than saturated fat. That is why all of our mothers were told to switch to margarine from butter. Another reason for hydrogenated oils' popularity is that they do not smoke at high temperatures. Therefore, they are perfect for fried foods like french fries. We now know that these hydrogenated oils increase cardiac risk, not decrease it, and have been shown to increase the risk of breast cancer. I have two rules:

Rule 1: Never eat anything that does not spoil easily.

Rule 2: Never eat anything that wild animals will not eat. (Just leave a tub of margarine out in your back yard and see if anything will eat it. Even skunks and ants will not touch it.

A study presented at the 2005 meeting of the *American Society of Clinical Oncology* showed that women who changed to a lower fat diet (about 30 grams per day) had a 24 percent lower rate of recurrence of breast cancer compared with women eating a higher fat diet (about 50 grams per day). Women with the hard-to-treat estrogen negative tumors received the most benefit, with a 42 percent reduction of recurrence compared with women who continued to eat a higher fat diet. Women with estrogen positive breast cancer had a 15 percent reduction of recurrence when they followed the lower fat diet.

This study confirms that a lower fat diet is not only important for breast cancer prevention but very important to reduce the risk of recurrence. As we discussed, it is important to eat the right type of fats, especially the omega-3 fatty acids (see below). These fats are very important for energy production, cell health, and brain function. The type of fats you want to reduce are the omega-6 fats, which are the most common fats used in the American diet (oil from corn, safflower, cottonseed, and soybean are all high in omega-6) Most margarine, mayonnaise, salad dressings, baked goods, and fried foods that you buy are made with these oils (an exception are those products made from canola or olive oil you buy at health food stores). Omega-6 fats increase inflammation, which may be one way they increase the risk of breast cancer. In years past, meat, eggs, and salmon were low in omega-6 fats, but now cattle, chickens, and salmon are fed corn, which is high in omega-6; therefore they become higher in omega-6 fats. (Try to eat free-range beef, chickens, and wild salmon). So the moral of the story is "change your oil"—reduce the amount of omega-6 fats in your diet and increase the amount of omega.[3]

Use Omega-3 Oils. These are the oils in ocean fish, flaxseed, and other seeds and nuts, including canola. We have already discussed how beneficial flaxseed and flax oil are in preventing breast cancer. If you are cooking at high temperatures (that is, sautéing or frying), then canola oil is the choice, since it does not smoke at high temperature. For everything else, use olive oil. Olive oil is technically an omega-9 fatty acid, but it has been shown to have many health benefits associated with it. Societies that use olive oil have lower risks of heart disease and cancer than Americans. In addition, olive oil has proved its health benefits for over 8,000 years, and it tastes great! Make sure you use organic, cold-pressed virgin olive oil.

Reduce Your Sugar Intake

Sugar intake has been linked with breast cancer in postmenopausal women.[3] You should keep your diet as low in refined sugar as possible. The best way to do this is by reducing your junk food. Commercially available pies, cakes, and candies all contain predominantly sugar. As we discussed before, many commercially available blueberry pies have very few blueberries and are mostly blue sugar syrup. You get the sugar without the antioxidants. (That's a pretty lousy deal!)

Get the majority of your sugar through fruit and fruit juices. However, if you have diabetes or hypoglycemia, you will not be able to eat as many servings of fruit or fruit juice as a "normal" person. You can compensate for this by eating more vegetables and/or taking an antioxidant supplement.

Consume More Soy

We have already discussed how beneficial soy can be for improving the detoxification of estrogen (that is, raising the 2 OH metabolite levels and decreasing 16 OH).

Eat Your Cruciferous Vegetables

We have also discussed how brussels sprouts, broccoli, kale, cabbage, turnips, collards, and cauliflower improve your EMI (2 OH/16 OH ratio).[4] Increase your cruciferous vegetable intake in every way possible. But avoid cruciferous vegetables if you are pregnant or breast-feeding.

Increase Your Antioxidants

We have reviewed how green tea and curcumin can slow the growth of breast cancer by inhibiting cell growth at two separate stages. Additionally, other spices, including rosemary, can enhance the metabolism of estrogen.[5] Therefore, include rosemary in as many dishes as possible.

Consume More Yogurt

We have reviewed how eating organic yogurt can help replace the normal bacteria in your bowel, thereby improving bowel function, reducing constipation, and allowing for better elimination of estrogen metabolites.

THE BOTTOM LINE

All of these dietary recommendations are so easy and so delicious. It would be a shame for you not to institute them, especially since doing so does not have to be time consuming or boring. There are delicious recipes available. Find the recipes that you enjoy and that taste good to you and utilize them.

Lastly, deprogram yourself from the TVcommercials. Remember, those commercials are there to sell a product and to make money. They are not there for the public interest or benefit. They are not designed to keep you from getting breast cancer. Throughout this book, we have discussed various nutritional supplements that can help improve your estrogen metabolism and reduce your risk of breast cancer. There are, however, nutrients in foods that we still have not discovered. The majority of your antioxidants and nutrients should come from your food. The addition of supplements will then allow you to bolster your antioxidant/nutrient intake. These two steps—improving your diet and choosing appropriate antioxidant/nutritional supplements—are a dynamic one-two punch to help you reduce your risk of breast cancer by 90 percent or more.

Determine If SERMs Are Right for You

SERMs are the only drug treatment that traditional medicine has available to reduce your breast cancer risk. The other treatment is to have a preventive double mastectomy—the removal of both breasts. This is the most radical possible treatment and one that most women would find unacceptable (though many women with very high risk factors consider this an option). SERM stands for selective estrogen receptor modulator. SERMs are prescription medications that can act like either an estrogen or an antiestrogen, depending on how they are designed and the tissue to which they are exposed. The two most common SERMs are raloxifene (Evista) and tamoxifen (Nolvadex).

TAMOXIFEN AND RALOXIFENE

As noted in the *Journal of Family Practice*, "At best using tamoxifen to treat 1,000 high-risk women for five years would prevent seventeen cases of invasive breast cancer and seven cases of noninvasive breast cancer, while contributing to at least seven uterine cancers and two pulmonary emboli."[1] Many women and their physicians have found the disadvantages of tamoxifen—including possible life-threatening uterine cancers, strokes, pulmonary embolisms, and uterine sarcomas—to be an unacceptable risk, given the fact that at best tamoxifen appears to reduce the risk of breast cancer by about 50 percent in women at high risk. Tamoxifen has no effect on women who develop estrogen receptor negative breast cancer and is not indicated in young women or women who are at low to moderate risk.

Raloxifene has been approved for the treatment of osteoporosis, and there are several studies that show that it does reduce breast cancer risk for those women at high risk. Additionally, it does not appear to increase the risk of uterine cancer, as has been noted with tamoxifen.

The disadvantages still include an increased risk of deep-vein blood clots (venous thrombosis), which have the possibility of developing into pulmonary emboli (blood clots that go to the lungs, potentially a life-threatening phenomenon). Raloxifene does not reduce postmenopausal symptoms; therefore, many women continue to have hot flashes, night sweats, sleep disturbances, cognitive dysfunctions, and other menopausal symptoms while on raloxifene.

For some women, raloxifene made the hot flashes worse. (It should be noted that for most women, this was a temporary phenomenon lasting for several months.) Raloxifene does appear to have more benign side effects than tamoxifen. That having been said, it still has increased risk of significant, possibly life-threatening side effects, including venous thrombosis. Therefore, it should be considered only for those women at a very high risk of breast cancer.

SHOULD YOU CONSIDER SERMS?

If you are at low to moderate risk for breast cancer, then you should institute the changes we have reviewed in this book. At this point in time, SERMs are not indicated for those of you in the low- to moderate-risk group. If you are in a high-risk group, then certainly you should institute the changes we have discussed in this book first.

There are several studies that indicate that nutrients such as I3C and DIM may actually improve the cancer prevention effect of SERMs. SERMs, however, are recommended for only five years of use; the longer you are on SERMs, the greater the risk of the side effects we have discussed. Many of my patients are very uncomfortable with SERMs and their possible side effects. I do not and have not prescribed SERMs, but certainly I have seen many patients who take these medications (prescribed by their gynecologists).

Whether or not to go on a SERM if you are at high risk is a difficult decision, one you must discuss very carefully with your doctor. I have very briefly discussed the advantages and disadvantages for those of you who may not be familiar with these medications and for those of you who have had SERMs presented to you as a treatment option but may not be familiar with the down side of these medications.

Unfortunately, it has been my clinical experience that the advantages are often explained to women in great detail, while the disadvantages are often underplayed. See Figure 18.1.

RALOXIFENE

Advantages

- Reduces breast cancer risk (claim not approved by the FDA).
- Approved for the treatment of osteoporosis.
- Does not appear to increase the risk of uterine cancer (a risk seen with tamoxifen).

Disadvantages

- Does not reduce menopausal symptoms, including hot flashes, night sweats, sleep disturbances, and/or cognitive dysfunction. May actually increase hot flashes.

- Increases the risk of venous thrombosis (blood clots of the veins).[2]

TAMOXIFEN

Advantages

- Approved for breast cancer prevention in high-risk women only.
- Approved for the treatment of breast cancer or metastatic breast cancer.

Disadvantages

- Warning of serious and life-threatening events with the use of tamoxifen, including increased risk of:

    - Uterine cancer
    - Stroke
    - Pulmonary embolism (movement of a blood clot to the lungs)
    - Uterine sarcoma

Figure 18.1 Advantages and Disadvantages of SERMs

Start Exercising to Lower Your Risk

Nearly every medical study shows that exercise lowers breast cancer risk. These studies show that walking just 1 hour three times per week lowers your chance of dying from breast cancer by 25 percent! In addition, the more intense the exercise (running rather than walking), the lower your risk. Studies have not confirmed exactly why women who exercise have a lower breast cancer risk, but there are several mechanisms that can explain how this happens.

EXERCISE REDUCES BODY FAT

Many studies have shown that women with higher levels of body fat have increased risk of breast cancer and a reduced chance of survival if they do get breast cancer. One reason for this is that fat produces estrogen. Interestingly, percentage of body fat is one way nature can judge if it's a good time for a woman to have a baby. As your level of body fat increases, you make more estrogen, which in turn improves a woman's chances of getting pregnant. This process makes sense when you look at it from an evolutionary perspective. Ten thousand years ago, there were no grocery stores, and starvation was a major problem. The last thing a woman needed was to have a baby during famine. Fortunately, the body has built-in mechanisms to reduce fertility during times of scarcity and improve fertility during times of abundance. When food was plentiful, a woman's body fat would increase and her estrogen levels would rise, improving her fertility (the right time to have a baby is when food is plentiful).

Fast-forward to Western societies in the twenty-first century, where food is everywhere and obesity is a national epidemic in America and many other Western societies. Nature interprets this as a perpetual state of abundance, so estrogen levels stay high for years because body fat stays high. As we've seen, these elevated estrogen levels increase risk of breast cancer, especially if you are not detoxifying estrogen properly. In the twenty-first century, we need to use a regular exercise program to keep our body fat under control because most of us don't walk miles as part of our jobs, and we certainly don't walk the 5 to 8 miles per day that native peoples used to walk as part of everyday living. Regular exercise programs lower body fat, therefore lowering estrogen levels and reducing breast cancer risk.

EXERCISE IMPROVES
DETOXIFICATION OF ESTROGEN

As a second mechanism for lowering breast cancer risk, regular exercise reduces constipation. We saw in Step 16 that many estrogen metabolites are removed from the body via the bowel. If we are not able to eliminate these waste products on a regular basis, an increased percentage will be reabsorbed back into circulation, increasing the stimulation to the breasts and increasing breast cancer risk. One of the first things any physician will tell a patient with chronic constipation is to begin a regular exercise program. Therefore, exercise improves the elimination of estrogen metabolites from the body, which lowers breast stimulation caused by those metabolites, therefore lowering breast cancer risk.

EXERCISE BOOSTS IMMUNITY

A third possible mechanism explaining why exercise lowers breast cancer risk is that even low levels of exercise improve your immune function. We have discussed natural killer (NK) cells and the vital role they play in detecting breast cancer cells and killing those cancerous cells in their earliest stages. We have also seen that the better your NK cell function is (within reason), the better your chance of killing the 200 cancers we develop every day and the better your chances of avoiding a serious tumor. Exercise improves NK cell function. Studies on some animals have shown that those animals that were walked around a ring just six times daily had a 50 percent improvement in immune function compared with animals that weren't walked. Many human studies also have shown that even mild exercise—as simple as walking up stairs at work instead of taking the elevator—can have positive effects on immunity. Throughout this book, we have focused on reducing breast cancer risk, but of course anything that improves immunity also reduces risk for nearly every other form of cancer, not to mention cardiac disease and serious infection. One study from the medical literature shows that exercise can reduce ovarian cancer risk by 33 percent.

HOW MUCH SHOULD YOU EXERCISE TO LOWER YOUR BREAST CANCER RISK?

The medical studies are not completely clear on just how little or how much exercise will maximize your breast cancer reduction, but this much we do know: walking 3 hours a week at a relatively slow pace of 3 miles per hour cuts your risk of dying from breast cancer by *25 percent*; walking 3 to 8 hours a week cuts your risk of dying from breast cancer in *half*! (This study was presented at the American Association for Cancer Research in 2004.) Clearly, walking at least 3 hours a week at a pace of at least 3 miles per hour is a great place to start. If you can't start at that level, don't worry. Just begin at a level where you feel comfortable, and increase the level or intensity of your exercise slowly. The key is to start at an easy level, increase the distance or pace slowly, and *keep at it*!

If you hate walking and find it boring, simply find a form of exercise you like—swimming, biking, tennis, golf (without a cart)—or use the gym. If you don't like the kind of exercise you do, you won't do it for long, so find the form of exercise that's right for you. If you like weight training for toning, that's great, but also include some aerobic exercise at least three times a week (aerobic exercise is anything that gets your heart rate up.)

THE BOTTOM LINE

- Start an exercise program and stick with it. The more years you exercise, the lower your breast cancer risk will be. Try to start walking—three times per week.

- Do a form of exercise you enjoy. If you don't like it, you won't stick with it.
- Start slow and increase your activity slowly. If you have health issues such as high blood pressure or heart disease, make sure you get clearance from your doctor.
- Find excuses to walk instead of riding. Park farther away from work or the mall. Use the stairs instead of the elevator. Walk down to the store instead of driving.
- If you live in a northern climate, find an indoor area to exercise during the winter.
- If you can afford a treadmill or stationary bike, then you can exercise at home (while you're watching your favorite TV show). If you can't afford exercise equipment or a gym membership, don't worry; walk in your local mall or high school.
- Add a sensible exercise program to the other steps we have shared in this book, and you will be well on your way to significantly lowering your breast cancer risk.

Putting It All Together

WHAT TO DO NOW

Learn Your Estrogen Quotient (EQ)

You must know your EQ! The 24-hour urine test for estrogen metabolism evaluation will tell you your EQ.

Remember:

$$EQ = \frac{\text{Estriol}}{\text{Estrone (E1)} + \text{Estradiol (E2)}}$$

If your EQ is less than 1.2:

- Consider changing your estrogen replacement therapy (ERT) to estriol (see Step 3).
- Add soy and flaxseed to your diet (see Step 6).

Learn Your Estrogen Metabolite Index (EMI)

You must know your EMI! Obtain this number from the 24-hour urine test for estrogen metabolism evaluation or separately from the urine EMI.

If your EMI is less than 2:

- Increase the cruciferous vegetables in your diet (see Step 4).
- Increase the soy and flaxseed in your diet (see Step 6).
- Consider supplementation of bioavailable DIM or I3C (see Step 5).

Repeat your EMI every 6 to 12 months until it reaches 2 or above.

Know Your Progesterone Levels

You must know your progesterone level! Obtain this through a saliva progesterone test, a urine test for free progesterone, or if your doctor will only do a blood test, then a serum progesterone level.

If your progesterone is low:

- Consider using a bioidentical progesterone cream (see Step 8).

Get a Bone Density Test

You must know your bone density! You can find this out by having your urine tested for bone loss markers or by having a dual photon densitometry of your lumbar spine, hip, and wrist.

If your bone density is low:

- Consider taking 2,000 milligrams per day of absorbable calcium.
- Take 400 IU of vitamin D daily.
- Take progesterone if your progesterone is low (see Step 8).
- Increase the soy foods in your diet.
- Consider taking black cohosh or estriol if not on estrogen replacement (if you have menopausal symptoms).
- Consider taking calcitonin or bisphosphonate (Fosamax, Actonel).
- Consider supplementing with boron and trace minerals.
- Retest your urine for bone loss in 6 to 12 months and your densitometry as directed by your health care practitioner.

Increase Your Antioxidants

To know your B_{12} and folate levels, ask your doctor for a blood test to measure your B_{12} and folate (see Step 14) or have your blood levels checked for methylmalonate and tetrahydrofolate.

If your B_{12} and folate levels are low:

- Consider taking 1,000 micrograms of B_{12} sublingual daily.
- Consider taking 1 milligram of folate daily.

Know Your Glutathione (GTH) Level

Know your glutathione level, and consider taking 500 milligrams per day of N-acetylcysteine (NAC) to help your body make GTH. Also:

- Add as many fresh organic vegetables to your diet as possible.
- Add green tea and turmeric as often as possible, and consider curcumin supplementation.

Detoxify

If your level of beta-glucuronidase is elevated, consider adding calcium glucarate and a probiotic (good-bacteria) supplement. Your beta-glucuronidase level can be determined by a special stool test. Along with giving you information about your beta-glucuronidase level, the complete digestive stool test will tell you if your bowel is overgrown with "bad" pathogenic bacteria or yeast. It will also give you the level of "good" bacteria.

THE BOTTOM LINE

By combining the steps we have discussed in this book, you will develop your personal breast cancer prevention plan, allowing you to significantly lower your breast cancer risk. By taking these active steps to take control of your life and your health, you will be well on your way to avoiding that personal "terrorist" we call *breast cancer*. Start with the easiest steps and build your program over time. Even if you don't follow every step and can only do three or four of these steps, you can still dramatically increase the chance that you and your family will not have to deal with this trauma. So don't put it off, for your sake and the sake of your loved ones, start today!

Notes and
General References

Introduction
1. "Failures of Estrogen Plus Progesterone Therapy for Prevention," *Journal of the American Medical Association* 288, no. 3 (2002).
2. Reuters News Agency report from meeting of the American College of Ob-Gyn (October 4, 2004).

Step 1
1. "Environmental and Heritable Factors in the Causation of Cancer," *New England Journal of Medicine* 343, no. 2 (2000).
2. L. C. Hartmann et al., "Efficacy of Bilateral Prophylactic Mastectomy in Women with a Family History of Breast Cancer," *Journal of American Medical Association* (June 27,1966): 1128–36.
3. J. C. Paschold et al., "Hereditary Breast Cancer and Update," *The Female Patient* 27 (2002): 13–24.
4. S. Narod et al., "Tamoxifen and Risk of Contralateral Breast Cancer in BRCA1 and BRCA2 Mutation Carriers," *Lancet* 356, no. 9245 (2000): 1876–81.

Step 2
1. J. V. Wright et al., "Comparative Measurements of Serum Estrogen," *Alternative Medicine Review* 4, no. 4 (1999).
2. H. M. Lemon et al., "Reduced Estriol Excretion in Patients with Breast Cancer Prior to Endocrine Therapy," *Journal of the American Medical Association* 196, no. 13 (1966): 112–20.
3. S. W. Fletcher et al., "Failure of Estrogen Plus Progestin Therapy for Prevention," 191, *Journal of the American Medical Association* 288, no. 3 (2002): 366–68.

Step 3

1. A. Lehninger, *Biochemistry,* 2nd ed. (New York: Worth Publishers, (1975): 681.
2. J. V. Wright et al., "Comparative Measurements of Serum Estriol, Estradiol, and Estrone in Non-Pregnant, Pre-menopausal Women," *Alternative Medicine Review* (1999): 266–70.
3. "Estrogen Therapy? Don't Worry!" *Life Extension Magazine* (October 1999).
4. H. M. Lemon, "Pathophysiologic Consideration in the Treatment of Menopausal Patients with Estrogen: The Role of Estriol and the Prevention of Mammary Carcinoma," *Acta Endocrinologica Supplementum* 233 (1980): S17–27.
5. H. M. Lemon et al., "Reduced Estriol Excretion in Patients with Breast Cancer Prior to Endocrine Therapy," *Journal of the American Medical Association* 196, no. 13 (1966): 1128–36.
6. V. A. Tzingounis, M. F. Aksu, and R. B. Greenblatt, "Estriol and the Management of the Menopause," *Journal of the American Medical Association* 239, no. 16 (1978): 1638–41.
7. T. S. Yang et al., "Efficacy and Safety of Estriol Replacement Therapy for Climacteric Women," *Chinese Medical Journal* 55:(1995): 386–91.
8. D. Perovic et al., "Treatment of Climacteric Complaints with Estriol" *Arzneimittelforschung* 25 (1997): 962–64.
9. G. P. Vooijs et al., "Review of the Endometrial Safety During Intravaginal Treatment with Estriol," *European Journal of Obstetrics & Gynecology and Reproductive Biology* 52 (1995) 62:101–6.
10. V. A. Tzingounis, M. F. Aksu, and R. B. Greenblatt, "Estriol and the Management of the Menopause," *Journal of the American Medical Association* 239, no. 16 (1978): 1638–41.
11. R. Punnonen et al., "The Effect of Oral Estriol Succinate Therapy on the Endometrial Morphology in Post-Menopausal Women," *European Journal of Obstetrics & Gynecology and Reproductive Biology* 14 (1983): 217–24.
12. C. Montoneri et al., "Effects of Estriol Administration on Human Post-Menopausal Endometrium," *Clinical and Experimental Obstetrics and Gynecology* 14 (1987): 178–81.
13. Minaguchih et al., "The Effects of Estriol on Bone Loss in Post-Menopausal Japanese Women," *Journal of Obstetrics and Gynaecology Research* 22 (1996): 259–65.

14. Mozakim et al., "Usefulness of Estriol for the Treatment of Bone Loss in Post-Menopausal Women," *Alternative Medicine Review* 3, no. 2 (1998): 105.

15. T. S. Yang et al., "Efficacy and Safety of Estriol Replacement Therapy for Climacteric Women," *Chinese Medical Journal* 55 (1995): 386-91.

16. G. B. Melis et al., "Salmon Calcitonin Plus Intravaginal Estriol an Effective Treatment for the Menopause," *Maturetas* 24 (1996): 83–90.

17. J. Hustin et al., "Cytological Evaluation of the Effect of Various Estrogens Given in Menopause," *Acta Cytologica* 21 (1977): 225–28.

18. G. M. Heimer et al., "Estriol in the Menopause," *Acta Obstetricia et Gynecologica Scandinavica* 139 (1987): 1–23.

19. G. Schar et al., "Effective Vaginal Estrogen Therapy on Urinary Incontinence in Post-Menopause," *Zentralblat fur Gynakologie*, 117 (1995): 77–80.

20. Razr et al., "A Controlled Trial of Intravaginal Estriol in Post-Menopausal Women with Recurrent Urinary Tract Infections," *New England Journal of Medicine* (1993): 753–56.

21. R. Punnonen et al., "Local Estriol Treatment Improves the Structure of Elastin Fibers in the Skin of Post-Menopausal Women," *Annales Chirurgiae et Gynaecologiae* 76, Supp. 202 (1987): 39–41.

22. J. B Schmidt et al., "Treatment of Skin Aging with Topical Estrogens," *International Journal of Dermatology* 35 no. 9 (1996).

23. J. L. Toy et al., "The Effects of Long Term Therapy with Estriol Succinate on the Hemostatic Mechanism in Post-Menopausal Women," *British Journal of Obstetrics and Gynecology* 85 (1978): 363–66.

24. K. A. Head, "Estriol: Safety and Efficacy," *Alternative Medicine Review*, no. 2 (1998).

25. C. Guo-jun et al., "Nystriol Replacement Therapy in Post-Menopausal Women," *Chinese Medical Journal* 106 (1993): 911–16.

Step 4

1. J. Schnieder et al., "Abnormal Oxidative Metabolism of Estradiol in Women with Breast Cancer," *Proceedings of the National Academy of Sciences of USA* 79 (1982): 3047–51.

2. J. Fishman et al., "Increased Estrogen 16-Hydroxylase Activity in Women with Breast and Endometrial Cancer," *Journal of Steroid Biochemistry and Molecular Biology* 20 (1984): 1077–81; D. W. Sepkovic et al., Estrogen Metabolite Ratios and Risks Assessment of Hormone Related Cancers," *Annals of New York Academy of Sciences* 768(1995): 312–16; R. G. Lahita et al., "Increased 16-Hydroxylation of

Estradiol in SLE," *Journal of Clinical Endocrinology and Metabolism* 53 (1981): 174–78.

3. E. N. Meilhan et al., "Do Urinary Estrogen Metabolites Predict Breast Cancer?" Guernsey III Cohort follow-up *Today's Journal of Cancer* 78, no. 9 (1998): 1250–55.

4. K. W. Luo et al., "Urinary 2/16 Hydroxy Estrone Ratio Correlation with Serum IgF BP3 as a Potential Biomarker of Breast Cancer Risk," *Annals of the Academy of Medicine Singapore* 27, no. 2 (1998): 294–99.

5. G. C. Kabat et al., "Urinary Estrogen Metabolites in Breast Cancer— A Case Controlled Study," *Cancer Epidemiology Biomarkers and Prevention* 7 (1997): 505–09.

6. "I3C The Tamoxifen Substitute: Cancer Prevention for Thinking People," *Life Extension Magazine* (October 1999): 28–34.

7. J. J. Michnovicz et al., "Cimetidine Inhibits Catechol Metabolism in Women," *Metabolism* 40 (1991): 170–74.

8. J. G. Liecht et al., "4-Hydroxylation of Estrogen as a Marker of Human Mammary Tumors," *Proceedings of the National Academy of Sciences of USA* 93 (1996): 3294–96.

Step 5

1. H. Bradlow et al., "I3C, A Novel Approach to Breast Cancer Prevention," *Annals of the New York Academy of Science* 76 (1993): 180–200.

2. "I3C The Tamoxifen Substitute: Cancer Prevention for Thinking People," *Life Extension Magazine* (October 1999): 28–34; J. J. Michnovicz et al., "Changes in Levels of Urinary Estrogen Metabolites After I3C Treatment in Humans," *Journal of the National Cancer Institute* 89, no. 10 (May 1997).

3. C. M. Cover et al., "Indole-3-Carbinol Inhibits the Expression of Cyclin-Dependent Kinase-6 and Induces a G1 Cell Cycle Arrest of Human Breast Cancer Cells Independent of Estrogen Receptor Signaling," *The Journal of Biological Chemistry* 273, no. 7 (1998): 3838–47.

4. Q. Meng et al., "Suppression of Breast Cancer Invasion and Migration by I3C," *Journal of Molecular Medicine* 78 (2000): 155–65.

5. I. Chen et al., "Indole 3 Carbinol and Diindolymethane as Aryl Hydrocarbon Receptor Agonists and Antagonists in T47D Human Breast Cancer Cells," *Biochemical Pharmacology* 51 (1996): 1069–76.

6. P. H. Jellinck et al., "Ah Receptor Binding Properties of Indole Carbinols and Induction of Hepatic Estradiol Hydroxylation," *Biochemical Pharmacology* 45 (1993): 1129–36.

7. C. A. DeKruif et al., "Structure Elucidation of Acid Reaction Products of I3C Detection in Vivo and Enzyme Induction in Vitro," *Chemico-Biological Interactions* 80, no. 3 (1991): 303–15.

8. C. L. Hayes et al., "17-beta Estradiol Hydroxylation Catalyzed by Human Cytochrome P-450 1B1," *Proceedings of the National Academy of Sciences USA* 93, no. 18 (1996): 7996–81.

9. M. A. Zeligs, "Safer Estrogen with Phyto Nutrition," *Townsend Letter for Doctors & Patients* 189 (April 1999): 83–88; "I3C The Tamoxifen Substitute: Cancer Prevention for Thinking People," *Life Extension Magazine* (October 1999): 28–34.

10. D. W. Sepkovic et al., "Catechol Estrogen Production in Rat Microsomes After Treatment with I3C, Ascorbigen, or Beta-Naphthaflavone," *Steroids* 59, no. 5 (May 1994): 318–23.

11. M. A. Zeligs, "DIM and I3C: The Real Facts on Safety" http://www.dimfaq.com/site/I3c-safety.htm.

Step 6

1. D. Ingram et al., "Case Controlled Study of Phytoestrogens and Breast Cancer," *Lancet* 350 (4 October 1997): 990–94.

2. H. Adlercreutz et al., "Excretion of the Lignans, Enterolactone and Enterodiol and of Equol in Omnivorous and Vegetarian Postmenopausal Women and in Women with Breast Cancer," *Lancet*, (11 December 1982): 1295–98; Ziegler et al., "Migration Patterns and Breast Cancer Risk in Asian-American Women," *Journal of National Cancer Institute* 85, no. 22 (17 November 1993).

3. A. Wu et al., "Adolescent and Adult Soy Intake and Risk of Breast Cancer in Asian-Americans," *Carcinogenesis* 23, no. 9 (September 2002): 1491–96.

4. X. Xu, A. M. Duncan et al., "Effects of Soy Isoflavones on Estrogen and Phytoestrogen Metabolism in Premenopausal Women," *Cancer Epidemiology Biomarkers and Prevention* 7, no. 12 (1998): 1101–8.

5. Ziegler et al., "Migration Patterns and Breast Cancer Risk in Asian-American Women," *Journal of the National Cancer Institute* 85, no. 22 (November 17, 1993.)

6. H. Adlercreutz, "Dietary Phytoestrogens and the Menopause in Japan," *Lancet* 339 (16 May 1992).

7. H. Adlercreutz. See note 6; H. Adlercreutz et al. See note 2.

8. X. Xu, A. M. Duncan et al., "Effects of Soy Isoflavones on Estrogen and Phytoestrogen Metabolism in Premenopausal Women," *Cancer Epidemiology Biomarkers and Prevention* 7, no. 12 (1998): 1101–08.

9. J. R. Lee, *What Your Doctor May Not Tell You About Breast Cancer,* (New York: Warner Books, 2002): 252–53.

10. R. Arnot, *The Breast Cancer Prevention Diet,* (New York: Little, Brown and Company, 1998): 59.

11. H. Adlercreutz et al., "Excretion of the Lignans, Enterolactone and Enterodiol and of Equol in Omnivorous and Vegetarian Postmenopausal Women and in Women with Breast Cancer," *Lancet* (11 December 1982): 1295–98.

12. S. M. Potter et al., "Soy Protein in Isoflavones: The Effects on Blood Lipids and Bone Density in Postmenopausal Women" *American Journal of Clinical Nutrition* 68, no. 6 (1998): 1375S–79S.

Step 7

1. J. B. LaValle, *Black Cohosh: A Natural Alternative Method for Balancing Hormone Levels* (New York: Avery/PenguinPutnam, 2000).

2. H. Stolze, "An Alternative to Treat Menopausal Complaints," *Gynecology* 3 (1982): 14–16.

3. G. Warnecki, "Influencing Menopuase Symptoms with a Phytotherapeutic Agent," *Medizinische Welt* 36 (1985): 626–29.

4. W. Stoll, "Phytopharmacon Influences Atrophic Vaginal Epithelium Double-Blind Study Cimicifuga vs. Estrogenic Substances," *Therapeuiticum* (1987): 23–31.

5. M. Muray, "Ask the Doctor," Vital Communications Inc. (1997).

6. E. Lehman-Willenbrock, "Clinical and Endocrinologic Examinations of Climacteric Symptoms Following Hysterectomy with Remaining Ovaries," *Zentralblatt fur Gynakologie* 110, no. 10 (1988): 611–18.

7. J. B. LaValle. See note 1.

Step 8

1. J. R. Lee et al., *What Your Doctor May Not Tell You About Breast Cancer* (New York: Warner Books, 2002).

2. J. M. Foidart et al., "Influences of Percutaneous Administration of Estradiol and Progesterone on Human Breast Epithelial Cell Cycle in Vivo," *Fertility and Sterility* 69, no. 5 (1998): 963–69.

3. K. J. Chang et al., *Fertility and Sterility* 63, no. 4 (1995): 785–91.
4. E. Cavalieri, "Estrogens as Endogenous Genotoxic Agents: DNA Adducts and Mutations," National Cancer Institute Symposium, March 1998.
5. L. D. Cowen et al., "Breast Cancer Incidence in Women with a History of Progesterone Deficiency," *American Journal of Epidemiology* 114, no. 2 (1981): 209–17.
6. L. D. Cowen. See note 5.
7. B. Formby et al., "Progesterone Inhibits Growth and Induces Apoptosis in Breast Cancer Cells Inverse Effects on Bcl-2 and p53," *Annals of Clinical and Laboratory Science* Nov–Dec 28, no. 6 (1998): 360–69.

Step 9

1. J. L. Freudenheim et al., "Premenopausal Breast Cancer Risk and Intake of Vegetables, Fruits, and Related Nutrients," *Journal of the National Cancer Institute* 88 (1996): 340–48.
2. D. J. Hunter, et al., "A Prospective Study of the Intake of Vitamin C, Vitamin E, and Vitamin A, and the Risk of Breast Cancer" *Journal of the National Cancer Institute* 329 (1993): 234–40.
3. Freudenhein et al. See note 1.
4. J. L. Freudenheim et al. See note 1; D. J. Hunter et al. See note 2; C. B. Ambrosine et al., "Interaction of Family History of Breast Cancer and Dietary Antioxidants with Breast Cancer Risk," *Cancer Causes and Control* 6 (1995): 407–15; S. Zhong et al., "Dietary Carotenoids and Vitamin C, A, and E and the Risk of Breast Cancer," *Journal of the National Cancer Institute* 91 (1991): 547–56; T. E. Rohan et al., "Dietary Fiber, Vitamin A, C, E, and Risk of Breast Cancer Cohort Study," *Cancer Causes and Control* 4 (1993): 29–37.
5. K. Nesaretnam et al., "Tocotrienols Inhibit the Growth of Human Breast Estrogen Receptor Status" *Lipids*, 33 (1998): 461–69; J. M. Turley et al., "Vitamin E Succinate Inhibits Proliferation of BT-20 Human Breast Cancer Cells," *Cancer Research* 57 (1997): 2668–75.
6. W. Yu et al., "Induction of Apoptosis in Human Breast Cancer Cells by Tocopherols and Tocotrienols," *Nutrition and Cancer* 33 (1999): 26–32.
7. M. Morrow, "Does Vitamin E Prevent Breast Cancer?" *Life Extension Magazine* (May 2002): 29–35.
8. M. Morrow. See note 7.
9. M. Morrow. See note 7.

Step 10

1. H. P. Ciolino et al., "Affect of Curcumin on the Aryl Hydrocarbon Receptor and Cytochrome p-450 1A1 in MCF-7 Human Breast Carcinoma Cells," *Biochemical Pharmacology* 56 (1998): 197–206.
2. *Life Extension Magazine* Abstracts (July 2002).
3. Hiroshi Inano et al., "Chemoprevention by Curcumin During the Promotion Stage of Tumorigenesis of Mammary Gland in Rats Irradiated with Gamma-Rays," *Carcinogenesis* 20, no. 6 (June 1999): 1011–18.
4. Hiroshi Inano et al., "Potent Preventive Action of Curcumin on Radiation-Induced Initiation of Mammary Tumorigenesis in Rats," *Carcinogenesis* 21, no.10 (2000): 1835–41.
5. R. Mohan et al., "Curcuminoids Inhibit the Angiogenic Response" *Journal of Biological Chemistry* 275, no. 14 (2000): 10405–12
6. Hiroshi Inano et al. See notes 3 and 4.
7. C. Jobin et al., "Curcumin Blocks Cytokine-Medicated NF-Kappa B Activation," *Journal of Immunolgy* 163 (1999): 3474–83.
8. S. Antony et al.,"Immunomodulatroy Activity of Curcumin," *Immunological Investigations* 28 (1999): 291–303.
9. R. Mohan et al. See note 5.
10. B. Aggarwal, "Tumeric Fights Breast Cancer in Mice," *Yahoo News* (June 10, 2005).

Step 11

1. *Epidemiology* (May 1991).
2. J. Kliukiene et al., "Risk of Breast Cancer Among Norwegian Women with Visual Impairment," *British Journal of Cancer* 84 (2001): 397–99.
3. E. J. Conley, *America Exhausted: Breakthrough Treatments of Fatigue and Fibromyalgia* (Flint, Michigan: Vitality Press, 1998).
4. S. Davis et al., "Night Shift Work, Light at Night, and Risk of Breast Cancer," *Journal of the National Cancer Institute* 93, no. 20 (October 17, 2001): 1557–62.
5. *Life Extension Magazine* Weekly Update (19 October 2001): 1–6.

Step 12

1. P. Toniolo et al., "Serum Carotenoids and Breast Cancer," *American Journal of Epidemiology* 153, no. 12 (2001): 1142–47.

2. K. Hulton et al., "Carotenoids, Alpha-Tocopherols, and Retinol in Plasma and Breast Cancer Risk in Northern Sweden," *Cancer Causes and Control* 12, no. 6 (2001): 529–37.

3. A. Khafif et al., "Quantitation of Chemopreventive Synergism Between (-)-epigallocatechin-3-gallate and Curcumin in Normal, Premalignant and Malignant Human Oral Epithelial Cells" *Carcinogenesis*, 19, no. 3 (1998): 419–24.

4. J. K. Lin, "Cancer Chemo Prevention by Tea Polyphenols" *Proceedings National Science Council* 24, no. 1 (2000): 1–3.

Step 13

1. A. Schecter et al., "Dioxins, Dibenzofurans, Dioxin-like PCBs and DDE in U.S. Fast Food," *Chemosphere* 34, no. 5–7 (1997): 1449–57.

2. "Beat the Odds Against Breast Cancer," *GreatLife Magazine* (October 2001): 32–35.

3. A. Schecter et al. See note 1.

4. A. Schecter et al. See note 1.

5. M. S. Wolff et al., "Blood Levels of Organochlorine Residue and the Risk of Breast Cancer," *Journal of the National Cancer Institute* 85, no. 8 (1993): 468–652.

6. T. Colburn et al., *Our Stolen Future* (New York: Penguin, Dutton/Signet, 1996).

7. M. S. Wolff et al. See note 5.

8. B. L. Smith, "Organic Foods versus Supermarket Foods: Element Levels" *Journal of Applied Nutrition* 45, no. 1 (1993).

9. Bradlow et al., "I3C: A Novel Approach to Breast Cancer Prevention," *Annals of the New York Acadamy of Sciences* 76 (1995): 180–200.

10. I. Chen et al., "I3C and DIM as Aryl Hydrocarbon (Ah) Receptor Agonists and Antagonists in T47D Human Breast Cancer Cells" *Biochemical Pharmacology* 51 (1996): 1069–76.

Step 14

1. Wu et al., "A Prospective Study on Folate, B_{12}, and Pyridoxal 5-Phosphate (B_6) and Breast Cancer," *Cancer Epidemiol Biomarkers and Prevention* 8 (1998): 209–17.

2. J. Soares et al., "Global DNA Hypomethylation in Breast Carcinoma," *Cancer* 85 (1999): 112–18.
3. "Vitamin B_{12} Deficiency: A New Risk Factor for Breast Cancer?" *Nutritional Reviews*, 57, no. 8 (1999): 250–53.
4. A. Pirisi, "Folate Acid Breast Cancer and Alcohol Consumption," Eurekalert press release, *Life Extension Magazine* (August 2001).

Step 15

1. A. M. Shamsuddin, "Inositol-phosphate Induced Enhancement of Natural Killer Cell Activity Correlates with Tumor Suppression," *Carcinogensis* 10, no. 9 (1989): 1595–98; A. M. Shamsuddin "IP-6: A Novel Anti-Cancer Agent," *Life Sciences* 61, no. 4 (1997): 343–54.
2. M. Ghoneum, "One Sizeable Step for Immunology, One Giant Leap for Cancer Patients," *Townsend Letter for Doctors & Patients* 198 (January 2000): 58–62.

Step 16

1. *Life Extension Magazine* (November 2000): 20; C. Dwivedi et al., "Effect of Calcium Glucarate on B-Glucuronidase Activity and Glucarate Content of Certain Vegetables and Fruits," *Biochemical Medicine and Metabolic Biology* 43 (1990): 83–92.

Step 17

1. S. Franceschi et al., "Intake of Macronutrients and Risk of Breast Cancer," *Lancet* 347, no. 9012 (18 May 1996): 135–56.
2. A. Wolk et al., "A Prospective Study of Association of Monosaturated Fat and Other Types of Fat with Risk of Breast Cancer," *Archives of Internal Medicine* 158, no. 1 (1998): 41–45.
3. "Beat the Odds Against Breast Cancer," *Great Life Magazine* (October 2001): 33–35.
4. J. H. Fowke et al., "Brassica Vegetable Consumption Shifts Estrogen Metabolism in Healthy Postmenopausal Woman," *Cancer Epidemiology Biomarkers and Prevention* 9 (Aug 2000): 773–79.
5. B. T. Zhu et al., "Dietary Administration of an Extract from Rosemary Leaves Enhances the Liver Microsomal Metabolism of Endogenous Estrogens and Decreases their Uterotropic Action in CD-1 Mice," *Carcinogenesis* 19, no. 10 (1998): 1821–27.

Step 18

1. "Does Tamoxifen Prevent Breast Cancer?—Clinical Inquiries," *Journal of Family Practice* 30, no. 12 (December 2001): 1023.
2. O. P. Phillips, "Raloxifene Versus Standard Hormone Replacement," *The Female Patient* 27 (May 2002).

General References

Atkinson, C. et al. "Effects of a Moderate Intensity Exercise Intervention on Estrogen Metabolism In Postmenopausal Women." *Cancer Epidemiology Biomarkers and Prevention* 13 (May 2004): 868–74.

Barnes S. et al. "Rationale for the Use of Genistein Containing Soy Matrices In Chemoprevention Trials for Breast and Prostate Cancer." *Journal of Cellular Biochemistry* 22 (1995): 181–87.

Bernstein, L. et al. "Physical Exercise and Reduced Risk of Breast Cancer in Young Women." *Journal of the National Cancer Institute* 86 (1994): 1403–08.

Cassidy, A. et al. "Biological Effects of Isoflavones in Young Women: Importance of Chemical Composition of Soybean Products." *Journal of Nutrition* 74 (1995): 587–601.

"Exercise Cuts Breast Cancer Risk." *WebMD Medical News,* February 10, 2003.

"Exercise: A Breast Cancer Nemesis." *cbsnews.com,* April 27, 2005.

Follingstad, A. H. et al. "Estriol, the Forgotten Estrogen?" *Journal of the American Medical Association* 239, no. 1 (1978): 29.

Head, K. A. "Estriol: Safety and Efficacy." *Alternative Medicine Review*, no. 2 (1998).

"I3C The Tamoxifen Substitute: Cancer Prevention for Thinking People." *Life Extension Magazine* (October 1999): 28–34.

Life Extension Magazine Abstracts (July 2002).

Index